inner
witch

A MODERN GUIDE TO
THE ANCIENT CRAFT

GABRIELA
HERSTIK

A TARCHERPERIGEE BOOK

tarcherperigee

An imprint of Penguin Random House LLC
375 Hudson Street
New York, New York 10014

First published in Great Britain under the title *Craft: How to Be a Modern Witch* by Ebury Publishing

Text photograghs by Alexandra Herstik
Line illustrations by Ollie Mann
Original birth chart from Rursus Wikimedia Commons

TarcherPerigee with tp colophon is a registered trademark of Penguin Random House LLC.

Most TarcherPerigee books are available at special quantity discounts for bulk purchase for sales promotions, premiums, fund-raising, and educational needs. Special books or book excerpts also can be created to fit specific needs. For details, write: SpecialMarkets @penguinrandomhouse.com.

Library of Congress Cataloging-in-Publication Data

Names: Herstik, Gabriela, author.
Title: Inner witch : a modern guide to the ancient craft / Gabriela Herstik.
Description: New York : TarcherPerigee, 2018. |
Identifiers: LCCN 2018019653 (print) | LCCN 2018022749 (ebook) |
   ISBN 9780525505341 | ISBN 9780143133544 (pbk.)
Subjects: LCSH: Wicca. | Witchcraft. | Feminism. | Magic.
Classification: LCC BF1571.5.W66 (ebook) |
   LCC BF1571.5.W66 H47 2018 (print) | DDC 133.4/3—dc23
LC record available at https://lccn.loc.gov/2018019653
p.   cm.

Printed in the United States of America
8th Printing

contents

INTRODUCTION

bitchin' witchin' basics

WE'RE WAKING UP.
AND WITH OUR
EYES TO THE MOON
WE RECALL THE
ETERNAL TRUTH.

YOU ARE A WITCH.

YOU ARE MADE
OF MAGICK.

IT'S TIME TO
REMEMBER.

Becoming a witch is an awakening, a remembering, an initiation. It's a chant to "come home, come home, come home," because even when you feel like you're lost, you're not.

From working with crystals, tarot and astrology, to solstices and full Moons, today's witches are integrating witchcraft and magick into their everyday lives. This is because as we navigate an incredibly charged cultural and political climate, we're left craving a deeper connection to something bigger. And for many women especially, witchcraft is a way to reclaim the divine in each of us, and a path that urges us to find a connection to the natural world, and to listen to how she affects us.

I have been a practicing witch for over a decade, but my journey started long before that, when my mother first gave me a crystal to hold to calm me down when I was upset with my twin sister. From there, my interest in the esoteric and occult grew, and my world changed forever when I received my first oracle deck, *The Faeries' Oracle* illustrated by Brian Froud. I became enthralled with the world of the faery, eventually picking up Edain McCoy's *A Witch's Guide to Faery Folk*, which took me back three years, to when I visited Salem and learned about witchcraft for the first time. After claiming the word "witch" at the tender age of twelve, I never looked back. Ever since then, I have explored what it means to be a modern witch, combining my love of clothing and fashion with a passion for magick and energy work. My belief is that by channeling ancient wisdom into the modern age, you are able to access the powerful, all-knowing, intuitive part of yourself regularly and easily. By living in tune with Nature and her cycles, you're more easily able to tend to your own cycles and needs as well. Being a witch means living in this world consciously, powerfully and unapologetically.

This book is my offering to the modern mystic who's looking to delve into witchcraft but who doesn't know where to start. May it act like the glossy September issue of the spiritual world, serving as a how-to for every woman looking to learn about what witchcraft is and how she can incorporate magick into her everyday life, without having to drop a million dollars. This book will cover the basics of witchcraft, and comes with plenty of spells and rituals so you can get your inner witch singing. More than anything, it aims to enrich your life by infusing the mundane with some magick.

Women run the world after all—and the ones who do are usually witches. This book is for them.

so, what *is* witchcraft?

Witchcraft is a Nature-based path that worships the Earth as the ultimate Mother, healer and Goddess. It's also a way to honor, learn about and explore all the beings and energies on this plane, even those that we may not be able to see with the naked eye. Witchcraft is magick—using intention, through spells and rituals, for a desired outcome. (Magick in our case is spelled with a "k" to distinguish our craft from the sleight-of-hand magic performed by stage magicians.) It's a path that teaches you to feel the unknown and the unseen; it's a new way of looking at life and, damn, does it feel good!

But magick doesn't look the same for everyone. Your practice will be tailored to where you live, your spiritual beliefs, your natural intuitive abilities and your interests and passions. Your path and your best friend's path won't look the same, but that's the whole point. Think of your practice as a magickal cocktail, like a secret recipe no one else can steal. As long as it's safe to drink and delicious for you, it doesn't really matter what everyone else is drinking. *Your magick does not need to look like someone else's magick to be valid,* and that's something I want to emphasize. This book isn't a prescription, it's an invitation to find your own path.

Adapt these words, spells and rituals as you see fit, honoring your own power and intentions; your magick is strongest when it comes from *your* soul. Witchcraft evolves with the land and its people, so witchcraft today doesn't look the same as it did fifty years ago, and it won't look the same in the next fifty to come. The cultures, geographic location and energetic makeup of an area will influence the form of magick practiced there too.

Through working with the Earth, tapping into our own ever-abundant source of knowledge and wielding this knowledge for a desired outcome, a witch is able to curate her craft for who she, or he, is. The best part is that you're already a witch. You don't become a witch; you remember you already are one. We all have the capability to live in tune with the Earth and her energies just as the ancient witches did. Of course, this is a skill that needs to be cultivated, but the seeds are already there: they just need to be tended to.

the witch

A witch is many things: the medicine woman, the slut, the one without children, the activist, the outcast. *The witch has always lived and will always live.* A witch is a healer, a woman in tune with her sexuality, someone who works with the Earth, anyone who abides by her own rules. Very often, witches were the protesters, the catalysts, the ones calling for justice and using all their tools, physical and otherwise, to create change. A witch has always been someone who refuses to abide by the societal constructs of the time. She is an outsider, rooted in her own decisiveness; the witch has always been a threat.

a very brief history

You can trace the history of witchcraft on cave walls in ancient lands, back to the days when life and death were locked in a daily dance. According to *The Spiral Dance*, a seminal text by the American writer and activist Starhawk, witchcraft began 35,000 years ago when hunters would connect to the herds of reindeer or bison on an energetic level, "calling" or tuning in to them, and a few of the animals would allow themselves to be caught as a sacrifice. These hunters were the first shamans, aware that every living thing in this realm is connected, no matter how subtly; and the first to recognize the dance of life, death and rebirth.

The oldest witches were those who honored the Earth and lived by the cycles of the Moon. In Eastern Europe, the Moon was carved from stone. In Western Europe, she was honored on cave walls through paintings of bison and horses. Records of the phases of the Moon were carved onto bone, and the Goddess was shown holding the bison horn, the sign of the crescent Moon. For the Yoruba people of Africa, the Goddess was worshipped as Oshun and Yemoja, the goddesses of love and feminine mysteries respectively. In China, she was Kuan Yin, Mother Goddess of prayers. She was everywhere, even though she had many different names. She was always personified as Mother Nature.

Settlements eventually grew into communities, and people started to share their knowledge about everything natural and magickal, eventually forming the first covens or groups of witches. The ancient witches celebrated the "great festivals": Equinoxes and Solstices, as well as the cross-quarter days between—the same holidays that many of today's witches celebrate, which will be discussed in Chapter 1.

But that all changed in 1486, when the *Malleus Maleficarum*, or "The Hammer of the Witches," by Dominican monks Heinrich Kramer and Jacob Sprenger, was published. This book was a witch-hunt manual that was to cast a shadow of terror over Europe for hundreds of years. Witchcraft became an offense punishable by death. Women healers, medicine men, wise women and especially midwives became the most persecuted people during the witch hunts. It wasn't until the Witchcraft Act of 1753 in Great Britain that witches were subject to imprisonment or fines instead of death—an act that wasn't repealed until 1951. And there are still witch hunts going on in different parts of the world today, like Tanzania.

Claiming the title of "witch" in the modern age therefore means remembering all those who have gone before you to allow you to be where you are today. It is our responsibility to shift the narrative of the witch, redefining who she is and reviving her ancient power; welcoming all who walk in her path without forgetting those who allowed us to be where we are.

bitchin' witchin' basics

magick

Energy is your best friend. It's always there for you, no matter what. Remember that old saying, "energy is neither created nor destroyed"? Well, that's true for magick as well. The energy in this Universe has always been and will always be; it's the song of life and the kiss of the Cosmos. It's not just electricity; it's your thoughts and your feelings too. It's the secret ingredient, and the soul, for working magick.

Magick is energy plus intention; it's a way to manifest a desired outcome or effect. Symbols, stories and ritual are the language of the subconscious, helping us access our unconscious mind, the part that manifests magick. Magick can be done in many ways, but is usually practiced through spell and ritual work. Yet magick is also subtle; it's when you talk to the Moon, or light a candle and sing "Happy Birthday." It's when you hear the flowers say they love you, and when you know to phone a friend before they ask you to.

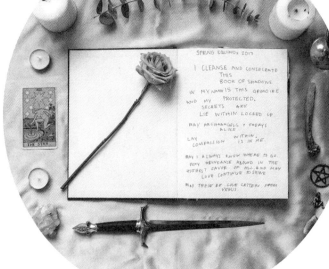

inner witch

Although some witches will call themselves "white witches" or say they work with "white magick" or "black magick," you will not see those terms in this book. Magick, at its very essence, is energy. And energy is neither black nor white, harmful nor helpful until the witch adds her own two cents and decides what it is. To call something that seems positive "white magick" and something that appears negative "black magick" is also inherently wrong. White attracts energy, both good and bad. Black repels energy, both good and bad.

One form of magick that I will also *not* be discussing in this book is any that aims to disrupt or dominate the free will of someone else. Acting against anyone's will inevitably leads to an inverse reaction, one that's deflected back at you. Using your magick to manipulate someone else is not a good look. And though there are times when this might seem necessary, this sort of magick needs to be worked with on a case-by-case basis. For instance, although performing love spells isn't advised because the results can be so unpredictable and messy, a binding spell (see pages 208–11) might help in the case of needing protection from somebody's negative vibes.

Finally the most important thing to remember about magick is that the power comes from the witch, and not the magickal objects themselves. *You* are magick. Yes, those crystals are beautiful and the tarot cards you bought do help you tap into your magick. But *you* are the Sun beaming through the magnifying glass that sparks the fire. *You* are the most important piece of the puzzle.

spells and rituals

Yes, being a witch means you get to cast spells! They won't be foolproof and they won't answer your wish in a matter of minutes, but spells are real and they work. A spell is an action that manifests a specific desire, usually with the help of a visualization, saying or chant, as well as magickal correspondences like herbs, candles or crystals. A spell shifts energy to change things and is equal parts intention, preparation, how you feel and the tools you have at hand. Oh, and that magic ingredient, love! Most of the time, when a witch casts a spell, she will cast a circle as a way to keep energy in and negativity out. Imagined as a sphere, the circle is a meeting way between worlds, where magick can be worked and energy can be raised in a safe setting. (See pages 45–47 for how to cast your own circle.)

And while we can confine spells to specific moments, we also cast spells of other kinds with our words and decisions each day. Those complaints you shared over lunch and those kind words you shared over coffee are both spells. It's all energy, remember?

Most of the time, a witch will work a spell within a ritual. A "ritual" is an umbrella term for a set of actions that takes place to connect us to something else, whether it's to our ancestors, to our hearts or to our unconscious. Rituals are moments that we can enjoy over and over again to create a sort of sacred pattern. Think of a ritual as including casting a circle, lighting herbs, grounding your energy (see page 29), invoking the Elements (more on that later)—and then casting a spell. Rituals are often longer and more involved than spells, and usually work by raising energy that's released in a cone of power, but sometimes rituals don't include spells at all. If a ritual is like a text you send to the Cosmos, then the spell is the words within the message of that text. Sometimes you'll send a gif or a meme, but most of the time you'll add some words too.

Different forms of rituals, and the basic steps of one, will be discussed in depth later on in this book (see pages 259–62). Before you do any spell or ritual, read through it at least once so that you familiarize yourself with the steps. At first it may seem overwhelming, but the format of every spell and ritual is the same, so it will get easier as time goes on. The spells and rituals throughout this book are meant to be a starting point. As you continue to develop your own practice, you'll start to develop a feeling for what works for you and for what doesn't. Honor this. Add things, take away things, research things. This is *your* craft, so use it how you see fit, honoring your intuition while you do so.

There are a number of things to consider when practicing magick that are important: the day of the week (since each day is ruled by a different planet and therefore has its own specific set of correspondences; see Tables of Correspondences, pages 274–77), and the actual tools involved such as cards, herbs, oils and even other energetic beings. But foremost are the intention of the magick itself and the desire and the willingness of the participant performing it. It really is like Professor Lupin said in *Harry Potter*: your feelings make the magick.

to join a coven or not to join a coven, that is the question

This book is meant to be a guide for the solitary practitioner: the witch who thrives in her own space, at her own pace and in her own time. It is an invitation to learn magick and then spread it as you wish, whether that's through gathering your mystical bffs for a new Moon sharing circle or reading cards with your significant other. Community is an important part of the craft, but it may not be your primary form of magick weaving.

All the same, that doesn't mean you can't or shouldn't join a coven. A coven is a group of, classically, thirteen witches who practice together and celebrate the witch's holidays of the sabbats and esbats together (which will be covered in the following chapter.) Although there are covens who practice the same form of witchcraft, and who are the offspring of a "mother" coven, each coven is its own entity and abides by its own rules and practices.

Choosing a coven is a personal decision, one which has to feel right to you. If you know you need a structured environment to thrive, and if you really value a community to help you learn, then you may very well decide to join a coven. But this isn't a decision you should take lightly, since being in a coven takes work. And it typically requires a commitment of a year and a day to become initiated. If you're committed to finding and joining a coven, you may want to see what options there are in your local community.

If you're somewhere between wanting to practice by yourself *and* in a super-structured environment, then you can absolutely form your own coven or witch support group with your friends. I have a group of friends who I practice with at the new and/or full Moon, and at the holidays. Sometimes we spend the day outside and at night we may perform something like a manifestation ritual where, after a short guided meditation, we share in a sacred space what we want to grow. This may include tarot readings, burning lists of whatever we want to release, and dancing.

You are free to create a practice and coven that works and feels right for *you*: your interests, loves and passions all have a place in your own form of witchcraft.

which witch are you?

There are various forms of witchcraft out there to suit different kinds of people, beliefs and interests. These include:

HEREDITARY WITCHCRAFT

Passed down from generation to generation. You'll probably already know if your family practices this path; think of family recipes with magickal ingredients, niche forms of divination and a family grimoire.

GREEN WITCHCRAFT

Works primarily with Nature as both an instrument and teacher. This path means living in alignment with the Earth and recognizing that everything has a spirit. A green witch works primarily with plants and herbs, gardening and growing. If you have a green thumb and a particular fondness for working with herbs and plant medicine, then you may be a green witch.

KITCHEN WITCHCRAFT

The natural calling for those who are adept at cooking, and who yearn to infuse their skill with some magick. Like other forms of witchcraft, you can incorporate aspects of this path into other traditions and practices. For the kitchen witch, spells and magick center on stove and hearth, with the process of cooking and eating acting as a form of ritual. By consuming the food you cook, you're releasing the energy into your own being and the Universe, forming an intention within yourself. Kitchen witchcraft is a good fit for holiday celebrations.

THE FAERY FAITH

Not to be confused with the Feri Tradition, which is another form of neo-paganism, this path of witchcraft works closely with energetic beings known as faeries or "the little people." The term "faery," or fey, refers to magickal beings such as sylphs, nymphs, undines, unicorns and pixies that are believed to exist in the astral realm—a realm parallel to ours. Those who subscribe to this practice believe that everything has a soul, even mountains, trees, flowers, oceans and rivers. They work with the thirteen lunar months of the Celtic tree calendar, accessing the different energies each month holds. Green witches and those who work with the fey often have overlapping practices.

WICCA

A neo-pagan, Nature-based religion that's loosely based on the beliefs of the ancient Celts. Wicca works closely with the Divine Feminine, or Goddess, and the Divine Masculine, or Horned God, in its rituals. Wiccans don't have a single holy book, but they do follow two laws: the Wiccan Rede, "an ye harm none, do what ye will," and the Rule of Three, "three times what thou givest returns to thee." There are many different sects of Wicca, such as Gardnerian, Alexandrian and Dianic, which all have different traditions.

CEREMONIAL MAGICK

Used in the context of Hermeticism and Western esotericism, ceremonial magick is a form of often secretive magick that incorporates long, complex rituals. The Hermetic Order of the Golden Dawn, which is a magickal order dedicated to the study and practice of occult and metaphysical matters, popularized ceremonial magick. Much like the Masonic Temple, the Hermetic Order of the Golden Dawn is based on initiation and hierarchy.

CHAOS MAGICK

A branch of magick that's more of a philosophy than a path. Sigils, or charged symbols, are a staple in this form of magick, which combines linking conscious intentions with the unconscious for a desired outcome. The end goal of a chaos magician is to master the subconscious in what's called a "gnostic state," whereby you can think and enact magick unknowingly. By using breathing techniques, muscle relaxation, sexual excitement or intense emotions, a practitioner of chaos magick is able to reach a state of gnosis.

ECLECTIC WITCHCRAFT

A combination of different practices that is unique to the practitioner. Eclectic witchcraft urges you to create your own path by drawing on your heritage, passions and different strands of magick. An eclectic witch might combine green witchcraft and kitchen witchcraft, art and music, or something else entirely. Eclectic witches are those who don't follow a single path;

instead they forge their own. (I count myself as an eclectic!) That said, if you follow this path, don't forget to be mindful of where you draw your inspiration and information from. Be respectful of the different cultures from which you learn and what they teach. Honor the ways in which their experiences may be different from yours—and make sure you thank whoever is teaching you.

CLEANSING WITH SACRED SMOKE

Using sacred smoke from herbs and plants is an ancient way to cleanse the energy of something, such as a space or person. The process is pretty simple but it's very potent.

While there are many different herbs and types of incense you can use to cleanse your space, below are some of the most popular, which can often be bought in prepared bundles from metaphysical shops:

» **White or Desert Sage:** helps get rid of negative energy and reset the vibrations of a room. Sage is sacred to many indigenous people and is overharvested because of high demand, which is making it harder for them to get access to it. If you choose to buy sage, make sure it's from somewhere that it's being ethically harvested. White sage is especially overharvested.

» **Palo Santo:** also known as "holy wood" and similar to sage, but a little less heavy duty. Helps clear the energy of a room and keeps energy grounded. This tree needs to die naturally for its power to remain, so make sure you're buying from somewhere ethical and reputable if you choose to work with this wood.

» **Cedar:** helps to purify a space/person, while grounding energy.

- » **Mugwort:** used to aid psychic visions and lucid dreams, and to clear out stuck negative energy.

- » **Sweetgrass:** invites in positive energy and spirits.

You can use an alabaster shell or bowl as a censer in which to burn your herbs, and a feather to help spread the smoke.

To cleanse a room:

- » Open any windows you can.

- » Start at the entrance of your space. Light your herbs and use the feather or your hand to fan the smoke.

- » Move around the room, making sure smoke gets into all the corners and crevices where stagnant energy might accumulate. Visualize the smoke clearing the space of any negative energy, and this energy being replaced with golden light. You can say, or think, something along the following lines:

  I cleanse and clear this space of any energy that isn't working in my highest favor. This is a sacred space that honors the highest good of all involved. May any negative energy move toward the light.

- » You can continue to the next room, starting at the door, getting into the corners and relighting the herbs if you have to.

You can cleanse a person in much the same way, making sure to waft smoke over their palms, throat, the crown of their head, soles of the feet, torso, arms and legs.

To cleanse an object, move it through the smoke of your chosen herb. This works for almost anything: grimoires, crystals, sacred ritual items, your phone, computer or television, etc. Get creative: anything that holds energy probably needs cleansing now and then.

You can cleanse a room or person anytime, but here are some particularly good times:

» After a full or new Moon or sabbat.

» After an energetically draining day or interaction.

» If someone you don't like has been in your space.

» When you're feeling overwhelmed emotionally.

» Before starting a new job or project.

witchcraft as self-care

Using witchcraft as a form of self-care means working with the elements of the Earth to feed and nurture yourself. Whether that's by finding peace through meditation, working with crystals that help you tune in to your heart, drawing a ritual bath to allow you to ground and center yourself or performing a banishing spell to get rid of unhealthy energies and relationships.

Being a witch doesn't mean there won't be days that will challenge you to your core or leave you feeling depleted. It just means that when these days happen you'll be more prepared for them, being able to see that everything is a cycle and that this too shall pass. A witchy perspective invites you to work with the energetic and physical tools at your disposal in order to (hopefully) take care of your whole being in a way that's often ignored by Western medicine.

Here are two simple ways to bring a little magick into your self-care routine.

TALISMANS

Work with a talisman, or an object charged with an intention. You can use a crystal, a pressed penny from the pier, a necklace your lover gave you or anything that has meaning to you and that's small enough to carry around easily. Jewelry works especially well as a talisman, as you can wear it.

Cleanse the object by smudging it, or leave it under the full Moon or in the blazing Sun. Sit with the object in your hands. Imagine the base of your spine as a golden cord connecting to the core of the Earth (see the "Golden cord method" on page 29 for more information about this). Then imagine a golden light at your heart growing bigger, eventually engulfing your entire body in glowing warmth. Focus your intention now, infusing it into your talisman. Maybe you want to keep your heart open, maybe you want to remember to be more compassionate to yourself. Either way, *feel* this. Remember a time when you felt loved, supported and cared for—and infuse that emotion into the talisman. When you're done, press your forehead into the Earth, imagining all the excess energy returning to her.

MANTRAS

You can also use mantras throughout your day as a form of self-care. They can be any affirming phrase that reminds you of your value. A few good ones include "I am worthy of every type of love," "I am a goddess," "I am loved, valued and appreciated" and "I choose to show up as my fullest self." You can repeat these every morning or at different points throughout the day. I've recently gotten into the habit of taping a list of mantras to my bathroom mirror and saying each mantra three times to my reflection each day. You can even set reminders on your phone so you don't forget. (Each day at 11:11 would be a great one!)

HEAVENLY ELEVEN

11:11 is an angelic number and doorway. The number 11 represents spiritual awakening and enlightenment, illumination and connection to our soul purpose. When we see the number 11:11 or 11 repeating, it's an invitation and reminder from our angels to pay attention to our thoughts and ideas. It's also a perfect time to make a wish or say a prayer.

witchcraft and sex

During the medieval witch hunts, women who were even the least bit comfortable with their sexuality were often deemed witches. A sexually liberated woman has always been seen as a threat to the patriarchy. However, witchcraft has always been sex-positive. Sexual energy is some of the most potent energy out there—connecting us to our Higher Self, the Universe and love.

Witches are accepting of all gender expressions and identities as well as sexual orientations; while we are all cut from the same cloth, modern witches recognize our differences as something to be celebrated. We also recognize that we are more alike than we are different. Sexuality is a natural, ancient part of our makeup, and as we evolve in consciousness, so must it. Witchcraft encourages you to embrace your sexuality and sexual energy, on the understanding that you aren't using it as a way to harm anyone.

A witch knows that sexual energy is life energy; the life–death–life energy has its root in our most primal, ecstatic state. Orgasm and the energy dispensed during sex and foreplay (with or without a partner) are some of the strongest and most unfiltered forms of energy there are; it feels good for a reason! The idea of a wo/man being dirty or sinful because of their sexuality isn't something witches abide by. Instead, witchcraft supports sexual exploration and figuring out what you do and don't like.

The Universe doesn't fit neatly into gender binaries either because gender binary is a man-made construct. The God is the personification of consciousness; of the part of us that is action-oriented; the part of us that shines like the sun, and nourishes the crops and works and plans and gets things done. This is the part of us that loves to accomplish, who wants to be dominant, who thinks with their head more than their heart. The Goddess is the personification of the subconscious; the part of us that is intuitive and feeling and emotional; the part of us that feels as deeply as the ocean, who hears the stars in the night, who feels the love of another before it is spoken. This soft, subtle energy is labeled as the Divine Feminine. These same forces can be described as yin and yang—the two opposite yet complementary energies described in ancient Chinese philosophy.

witchcraft as empowerment

Witchcraft teaches new ways to honor your needs, because it's a direct path to *harnessing your power*. For women (myself included) raised in environments that attempt to take away our bodily integrity and personal autonomy, witchcraft is a form of direct personal resistance. It's like playing by another set of rules that no one else knows about. It's a way to take back power while connecting to something larger than ourselves.

It's empowering to understand how things like the phase of the Moon, the workings of astrology and different periods of the year impact your personal energetic makeup. Knowing when and how to work with these cycles is liberating and shapeshifting.

There are those who would try to convince us that women and femmes (a queer person who expresses themselves in a traditionally feminine way) of all types are inferior; who attempt to convince us that to be "the ideal woman" we need to invest in new beauty products and clothing, in plastic surgery and all sorts of things that will make us more palatable, less wild and easier to digest. But of course, this isn't true. If a wo/man knows her worth and refuses to dim her light for anyone, there really isn't anything she cannot do.

WITCHCRAFT TEACHES NEW WAYS TO HONOR YOUR NEEDS, BECAUSE IT'S A DIRECT PATH TO HARNESSING YOUR POWER

witchcraft as spiritual activism

To change the outer world, we must begin in our inner world. This is the basis of spiritual activism; a way to shift your internal universe to be more open, receptive and involved in making a palpable difference in the physical realm. Magick can be used to help shift our own lives, creating a new space for us to inhabit that offers more of what we want, whether it's a space that's more creative, conscious, artistic or accepting.

Being a spiritual activist means acknowledging we are connected to all other beings in spirit and turning compassion into action. Witchcraft asks us to step out of our ego and into the consciousness that all of us inhabit together, working from a place that also serves *all of us*. Spiritual activism is a way of remembering that harming someone else ultimately means harming yourself. It doesn't necessarily mean you're going to change the world with one incantation; but it very much means the energy you work with acts as a ripple of light that touches every corner of the world in one way or the other. It works as an internal foundation for real-life activism.

combating spiritual materialism

Owning every book, herb, crystal and tarot deck there is will not make you a more powerful witch. Power comes instead from your mind, spirit and soul. Combating spiritual materialism means being conscious of what you buy, from whom you buy it and why you're buying it. Absolutely do purchase something if it feels right and you have the means, or if it's required for a spell or ritual. But don't feel like you need to spend huge amounts on that one herb for that one spell if it's way out of your budget. And don't feel like you need five of every stone and three cauldrons: just like having a million bottles of paint won't make you a painter, having every witchy object out there won't make you a witch.

Utilizing secondhand and vintage shops, local metaphysical and natural stores and online sites like Amazon, eBay and Etsy is one way to make sure you don't spend too much money on what you really need. Having a meaningful relationship with each item you purchase *will* make your magick more powerful. But the old adage of quality over quantity still rings true.

To work with the spells in this book, you'll need a few basic items as well as some that are tailored to specific spells or rituals. My goal is to give you access to tools you can use in new ways that feel good. And, like the rest of this book, the process of finding and working with your chosen items will be unique to you. *YOU are the most powerful tool you will ever need, and, honey, that magick don't cost a thing!*

start at your roots, plant your own seeds

More than anything, this book encourages you to find a path that's uniquely yours. This is the way of the witch and it asks you to engage with your origins, maybe even going far back through generations to learn about your own branch of magick. Do you know where you're from? Where your great-great-grandparents lived? Centuries ago, most people lived in tune with the Earth. There's a specific sort of magick that runs through no one else's blood but yours. The goal for you is to find this song, learn the melody and discover your own harmony. Learn about the family recipe for headaches that your mom has been making for you since you were little. Ask about the old superstitions your father swears by, or what sort of herbal remedies your grandparents know. Witchcraft, folklore and folk medicine go hand in hand.

Well, witches, now you know what to expect! Living in tune with Nature, finding your own style of spiritual self-care, working with energy and manifesting your future are all part of your destiny. Becoming a witch entails shouldering the responsibility given to us by generations of women who were persecuted for their beliefs; by recognizing this privilege, and working our magick, we're able to own our power as witches.

Witchcraft is about spells and rituals and magick—but it's also more than that. When we create a practice that fits into our lives and that allows us to live as a witch every day, not only are we able to help our own spirit grow and connect to our higher calling, but we're able to help others step into their power as well.

GROUNDING

Grounding is a way of creating a connection with the Earth both as a support system and as an abundant and never-ending supply of energy. Before any kind of ritual or magick work, a witch grounds her energy, and once she's done, she will return this energy back to the Earth, closing the channel and grounding her energy once again. Failing to ground energy after performing magick can leave you feeling anxious, tired, energetically depleted and more open to psychic attack.

Before performing magick, do one of the following grounding exercises:

GOLDEN CORD METHOD

Find a comfortable seat, close your eyes and take a few deep, intentional breaths. Be aware of your belly expanding as you breathe in and sense it contract as you exhale. Once you feel settled, imagine a golden cord extending from the base of your spine into the core of the Earth. Imagine the energy from the Earth finding its way up your spine, to your heart. Perhaps it will feel warm and radiant as it moves. Savor this connection. Know that you are supported. This is your lifeline, a support system that is always there.

TREE MEDITATION (INSPIRED BY STARHAWK)

Find a comfortable seat, close your eyes and take a few deep, intentional breaths. Feel your belly expand as you breathe in and contract as you exhale. Once you are settled, imagine the base of your spine as roots that dig deep into the Earth. Feel the energy traveling up your spine with each breath, like sap rising through a tree trunk. Savor this supported, grounded energy. Imagine this energy extending from the top of your head, sweeping back down to touch the Earth. Feel this circular energy moving through you. You have a few options on how to return your energy and ground your power too. Again, take time to feel the energy finding its way back into the Earth.

After performing magick, do one of the following grounding exercises:

INHALING METHOD

Find a comfortable seat, close your eyes and take a few deep, intentional breaths. Feel your belly expand as you breathe in and feel it contract as you exhale. Once you are settled, suck in your power as if you were sucking through a straw, feeling it flow through you back into the Earth.

SINKING INTO THE GROUND

Either lying down with your palms on the ground, or in the resting position known as the child's pose in yoga (kneeling forward with your forehead on the ground), take a few deep breaths. Relax and melt into the Earth. Feel the power sinking back into the Earth, imagining this to be so even if you're on the fifteenth floor! Let this energy flow deep into the Earth, starting from the top of your head and moving down your spine. Imagine this energy being cleansed and renewed in the core of the Earth.

create your own grimoire

The very word "grimoire" evokes a mystical vision of a witch clad in black, with the Moon's rays illuminating the scene. Before her is a leather book—her grimoire, or Book of Shadows—inviting her to spill her most treasured magick and secrets into it. The grimoire serves as the witch's magickal diary. Inside it, she records her spells, rituals, visions, correspondences for each day (like which particular planets, herbs and crystals are associated with the days of the week), tarot spreads, energy work (such as healing, meditations, trance work or crystal work), celebrations and more. This is what "completes" her, allowing her to build her own school of magick, with all the trial and error that occur along the way.

The most important thing to keep in mind when choosing a grimoire is to consider what works best for you in terms of organization. If you like, you can keep everything written down virtually on an app like Evernote, or in a Word document. You could also handwrite everything in a binder, adding and changing pages with ease. Or you can use a leather journal for that old-school witch feeling.

CONSECRATING YOUR GRIMOIRE

Although not every witch chooses to consecrate their grimoire, I love the intention of blessing the book, as well as the process of clearing it of any negative energy. To do this, you will need herbs for smudging as well as herbs to burn (sage or palo santo are good choices), a match or lighter, a little bit of water (or holy water, for which you can find the recipe in Chapter 8), your grimoire and something to write with. Try to do this ritual on the new Moon, although the waning Moon works too.

Step 1: Cleanse.

First, cleanse the space by smudging and use one of the grounding exercises on pages 29–30. Cleanse your grimoire with the sacred smoke as well.

Step 2: Consecrate.

Next, grab your incense or herbs. Say:

> *"I cleanse and consecrate this book in the name of the Universe and my highest truth. Through the power of Earth . . ."*

Light the incense or herbs, and say:

> *"Through the power of Fire . . ."*

while feeling the passion and warmth of Fire.

After blowing the flame out, run the book through the smoke and say:

> *"Through the power of Air . . ."*

while feeling the cleansing energy of this Element.

Dip your fingers in the water and splash droplets at the book while feeling the fluidity of the Element, and say:

> "Through the power of Water, we call upon the ancient and divine power. In this grimoire, magick I will write. Cleanse and consecrate this book tonight."

Step 3: Charge it with light.

Place your hands over the book, close your eyes and imagine a white light shining from your palms, surrounding the grimoire.

Step 4: Ground and write.

You can ground your power now or go on to the next step by writing a blessing on the first or second page of the grimoire. You can write whatever you want and dedicate it to whichever deity you feel called to, asking them to protect your book and magick from prying eyes. For example, you can write:

> "I bless this book in [your name*]'s highest favor,
> With the ancient magick found in these pages.
> The Universe wills it and so I create;
> May prying eyes fail to reciprocate.
> Earth, Air, Fire, Water—
> Elements, I ask on this ancient, ready hour
> To bless and protect me and these words,
> May they always feel like coming home.
> So it is, so it shall be."

---

*Some people prefer to use a magickal name for all their workings, and for their grimoire. Many incorporate elements from the natural world. If you feel inclined to create and use a magick name, please do!

CHAPTER ONE

what witches believe

Being a witch is about freedom. Freedom to be who you are, to grow as you wish, to worship in the way that you desire. There isn't a single book or law you have to believe in that officiates your initiation into the world of witch. But there are certain cosmic rules or laws that we acknowledge, which allow us to grow as magick makers and bewitching weavers.

We don't imagine God as being a giant man in the clouds. God—or the force I prefer to call the Universe—is also known as the Goddess, the Source, Creation and many other names; it is our essence.

She may wear many faces, or none at all. This force is bigger than we are; why would we put human qualities and characteristics on something that's not human? It is part of us, and we are part of it. It's from where we came and to where we shall return; it's the purest form of our soul and more. The language of the Universe is the feeling of being in love, of seeing the stars on a dark night, or of smelling fresh roses, and much more.

working with your karma

We all know Karma. She's the one friend who never leaves us alone. Who comes over sometimes at the perfect time (like when she randomly lends you that dress you were gonna ask about) and then also manages to find you at the most inconvenient times (like when she needed your help when her dog fell sick and you were on your way to a date). And while we love holding grudges against her, she always manages to teach us something important, so we can't get too mad.

Karma's not a bitch. She's *that* bitch. If you struggle against her and what she's teaching you, it's only going to get harder. But if you recognize her for what she is—a magnified mirror reflecting back your own stuff—then the rest of the lessons get easier.

Just as Newton's third law of motion states that for every action there is also an equal and opposite reaction, Karma says the same thing. Except in our case, this means that the energy you put out in the Universe at a spiritual, emotional, mental or physical level will come back to you in some way. Positive inspires more positive, and negative inspires more negative.

Karma is just, though we may not always see it. Karma can take generations to heal or generations to wound. We have personal karma: how we act and live in this life, generational karma, the karma of our families, and cultural karma: the karma of a region or society. These all interplay in different ways in our lives, and carry over from our past lives too.

life after life

Each witch will have her own beliefs about death, the afterlife and heaven, which is known as the Summerland in some neo-pagan traditions and Nirvana in some Eastern traditions. This is a notion that will probably evolve along with your practice of the craft, with there being no single "right" answer to the question of life after death. Personally, I believe in reincarnation or the idea that the soul is reborn life after life. Karma is reincarnation over time; we are born as many times as we need to be, until our souls become as pure and close to our true essence—and the Universe's essence—as possible. A belief in reincarnation is common among witches; however it's not universal, and not believing in reincarnation doesn't make you wrong.

your cosmic team

Time doesn't exist beyond this world. Our loved ones who have died can stay and assist us through our lives in the form of spirit guides, much like the idea of guardian angels. Spirit guides can be your ancestors from this life, or they can be guides from past lives. They can even be figures that you admire and look up to, who inspire you and have taught you in some way.

There are also ascended masters. They're like a spirit guide upgrade; they've fully broken free from the cycle of karma and death and rebirth, so they really know what's up. They're there for us in times of intense spiritual and emotional turmoil. While our spirit guides may help us in day-to-day life, the ascended masters help us in things that involve the bigger picture of our lives, which is often spiritual in nature.

Working alongside your spirit guides and masters are your angels. While the idea of angels may have Judeo-Christian connotations, angels are actually nondenominational beings who work to bring peace and love to us—the creatures of the Universe. They, like our other spirit guides and masters, are simply a call away.

Angels, spirit guides and ascended masters are like a team of cosmic cheerleaders and teachers who are here for you whenever you feel disconnected, alone, anxious or unsafe. Talk to them! I talk to my guides in the bathroom at work, in my car and when I'm walking down the street. They are with you for a reason, and even though it may take a second to learn their language, you can! Ask for signs, and invite their help in. Make art for them, decorate an altar and don't forget to talk to them.

MEDITATING TO MEET YOUR COSMIC TEAM

If you want to meet your cosmic team, you can meditate with them and invite them to make their presence known. You can use crystals like amethyst, angel aura quartz, clear quartz, angelite or celestite to assist you in accessing your guides.

Cleanse your space with sweetgrass or mugwort, and then find a comfortable seat. You can hold a crystal in your nondominant hand, or place it near you.

Start to ground your energy, focusing on your breathing as you imagine a door at the crown of your head opening.

Invite your cosmic team to make their presence known. Call on your spirit guides, angels, animal guides and benevolent beings, inviting them to show their presence.

Continue to focus on your breath, noticing if any messages, feelings, colors, smells or voices come up. When you're finished with the meditation, thank your team, imagine the door at the crown of your head shutting and ground your energy.

INVITING IN THE ELEMENTS

The Elements (or Elementals) are our connection to Nature and the Earth, as well as part of our emotional makeup. By inviting in Earth, Air, Fire and Water for magickal work, we are forming a relationship with these archetypes and energies, as well as the natural world. Water represents our emotional body, Fire represents our passion, Earth represents what supports us and keeps us safe and Air represents our creativity, dreams and desires.

You'll need: herbs such as palo santo, copal, sage or mugwort; something to light them with; and a chalice or bowl of water.

Ground yourself (see the exercises on pages 29–30) and connect to the Earth. As you begin this invocation, connect to the energy of each Element. Start by calling on Earth while imagining that you're lying in a field atop the grass. When you connect to Air, feel the wind kissing your cheek. As you call on Fire, imagine feeling warmed by a fireplace or bonfire. When you call on Water, visualize swimming in a pool of healing water.

Next, take the herb in your hand and say:

> *"Element of Earth, I call upon you and invite you into this space. May I always feel your support and protection."*

Light the herb and blow out the flame (if there is any) and move the herb so the smoke fills the space and say:

> *"Element of Air, I call upon you and invite you into this space. May I always feel your presence guiding me and supporting my flight."*

Light the herb again so there's a flame (if possible), and as you do, say:

> *"Element of Fire, I call upon you and invite you into this space. May I always see your light and feel your passion."*

Take the chalice of water and say:

> *"Element of Water, I call upon you and invite you into this space. May I always feel my intuition and your calming waters."*

You can either dip your herbs in the water, or sprinkle water from the chalice onto your herbs.

Take a second to sit with these Elements, receiving their energy and their blessing.

Proceed to your magickal work, meditation or divination.

When you're done with your spell or ritual, and feel called to dismiss the Elements, you'll take similar steps as before, but starting with Water and then dismissing Fire, Air and finally Earth.

Dip your fingers into the water and press it on the space between your eyes and say:

> *"Element of Water, I thank you for your blessing and energy, and I dismiss you from this ritual."*

Light your herb from before and say:

> *"Element of Fire, I thank you for your blessing and energy, and I dismiss you from this ritual."*

Wave your herb through the air so smoke fills your space and say:

> *"Element of Air, I thank you for your blessing and energy, and I dismiss you from this ritual."*

Put out the herbs and say:

> *"Element of Earth, I thank you for your blessing and energy, and I dismiss you from this ritual."*

Ground your energy by pressing your forehead into the Earth or by sitting in a cross-legged position. Imagine all the excess energy in your body and the room moving back into the core of the Earth, to be recycled and transmuted into love and healing. Thank the Elements and write down any feelings that may have come up.

how to cast a circle

You can't be a full-fledged witch without learning the basics of casting and closing a circle! Think of the circle as a sphere that surrounds you and your work completely. It keeps the energy you've raised inside it and any negative energy out.

There are different methods for casting a circle, but the most important thing is to find one that resonates with you. Here are a few ways to figure out your own circle casting style.

casting the circle

The circle should encompass whatever space you need to perform your spell or ritual, including your altar or whatever surface you're working on. For a solitary practitioner, this area should measure around six feet in diameter.

Before you cast a circle, make sure that you won't be interrupted and that you have everything you need. Take a second to ground yourself (see pages 29–30) and burn incense or herbs to help cleanse your space. Imagine you're surrounded by white light that comes from the heavens and descends upon you.

» When you're ready, walk in a clockwise direction (also known as deosil) around the space you want to encompass, starting by facing North.

» Use your finger, a wand or an athame (ritual knife), and imagine a bluish-white light extending from your fingertip or the object to form a protective hedge around you wherever you point.

» Walk the circle once or three times, while imagining the bluish-white light extending into a sphere above your head and below your feet.

» You can also physically mark the exterior of your circle with shells, crystals or salt. Salt is one of the smallest natural crystals and absorbs excess energy.

» When you've circled and returned to the front, you can say something like the following:

> "I cast this circle in perfect love and perfect trust as a meeting place between worlds. May this boundary protect and hold my energy."

» Once you have cast your circle, you should do your very best not to leave it while you are working, because the energy will dissipate if you do. However, if it's necessary to leave the circle, you can cut an energetic door into the circle, and pass through this so as to not disturb the surrounding energy.

» To cut a doorway, you can use your finger, wand or athame to mimic "cutting" a doorway into the circle, rising up from the ground, above your head, to the side and then down again.

Step through the door, and try to do what you need to do quickly. You can reenter the circle through the same doorway, recutting it if you wish. If you have to be gone for more than ten minutes, it might be best to recast the whole circle.

closing the circle

Close the circle the same way you cast it, after your ritual or spell is complete. Except this time you will walk in a counterclockwise direction (or widdershins) to close it, instead of clockwise.

» Using whatever tool you used before, imagine the energy you cast coming back to you, through your body, through your feet back into Mother Earth. Walk once counterclockwise around the circle before stopping at the front of where your circle was, and say:

"The circle is open, may it never be broken."

» Ground your energy by pressing your forehead and palms to the floor, imagining any excess energy returning to the Earth.

As your magick starts to grow in strength, you may find a better way to cast your circle. Perhaps you will do yours seated or during meditation, imagining a giant bubble filling up with golden white light that surrounds you. Perhaps you make up your own prayer or song to sing as you're casting your circle, using a candle at each corner to mark the boundary.

Traditionally, to open the circle you walk clockwise, or deosil, and to close it you walk counterclockwise, or widdershins. It's up to you to find the method that makes you feel the most protected, safe and supported.

AS ABOVE, SO BELOW. AS WITHIN, SO WITHOUT. THERE ARE LAWS EVERY WITCH SHOULD LEARN ABOUT.

the universe and witch's laws

All that we see and experience is but one aspect of the Universe. The Universe is divided into levels, each composed of energy in a different way. And while we live in a level ruled by our senses, this is only one plane of reality. If our Universe were an onion, then our level would represent a single layer. As we move higher and higher through the layers of the onion, they become less dense—just like the Universe moves away from the physical toward the energetic.

I will be talking about the astral realm in more detail later in this book. This is the realm parallel to our own, where the faeries and other Nature spirits, like sylphs, nymphs and unicorns, exist. It is where we find ourselves when we have a lucid dream. It's where our ancestors come from to talk to us.

First, we must remember the laws of the universe that allow us to work our magick. Understanding these spiritual and energetic laws will help us learn how to work with the universe to allow our magick to unfold as effortlessly as possible.

As above, so below. As within, so without. There are laws every witch should learn about.

Law	Meaning	Example
Sympathetic Magick	An umbrella term for magick that imitates its desired outcome.	See the Law of Similarities and the Law of Contact below.
Law of Similarities	Like attracts like; to elicit a certain outcome, you imitate the outcome you desire.	Working with the waxing (new to full) Moon to manifest, and with the waning (full to new) Moon to banish and release.
Law of Contact	Two things that have been in contact will keep interacting energetically at a distance.	Using a piece of someone's hair or clothing for a spell even if they're not present.
Law of Least Effort/ Resistance	As Nature happens effortlessly, so do we. The more we let go of a desired outcome, the more likely it is to happen.	When you can't stop thinking of someone and they haven't texted you. As soon as you move on or stop caring, they text you.
As Above, So Below. As Within, So Without.	Everything happening out in the Universe is also happening to us. The microcosm is the same as the macrocosm.	The nucleus to the rest of its cell is the same as the Sun to the solar system.
Karma/The Rule of Three	What we give, we get in return. Three times what you send out comes back to thee.	Helping your friend through a rough breakup and then getting asked out on a date.

symbols of the witch

Each witch shall have her proper symbols that help her tell who she is. These are some of the most common magickal items and symbols associated with the craft. You can incorporate the symbols into your grimoire or buy the items for your altar and your practice. Find what speaks to you and work with it.

PENTACLE

One of the most prominent symbols in witchcraft is the pentacle. A pentacle is a pentagram, a five-pointed star, enclosed within a circle. Each point in the pentagram represents an Element: Earth, Air, Fire and Water, with Spirit at the top. Spirit, aka the Universe, is on top because that's the thread tying the other Elements together. The circle enclosing the pentacle represents this thread, this universal consciousness that runs through the Earth around us and inside us, connecting it all together.

Invoking

Banishing

THE TRIPLE MOON

The Triple Moon is symbolized by a
waxing and waning Moon on either side of a full Moon. This
symbol is said to represent three aspects of the Goddess:
maiden, mother and crone, which are archetypes undefined by
time or necessity (like actually being a mother, or being young or
old). This symbol is associated with feminine mysteries, Goddess
worship, psychic protection and the Divine Feminine.

THE CAULDRON

Inspired by Celtic legend, the cauldron
symbolizes the Goddess and the womb from
which all life comes. This is one of the most ancient symbols of a
witch, representing her inherent connection to the Divine
Feminine while also representing her power for physical and
energetic manifestation. At the cauldron, the witch is able to
create life-affirming foods, stews and potions; she's been able to
divine the future, burn sacred herbs and create and cast spells.

THE CHALICE

The chalice, or cup, is another symbol associated with the Divine
Feminine, with the flow of emotions and the womb. The chalice
can be kept on the altar or stored away wrapped in a black cloth.
The chalice is used to represent the Divine Feminine and to leave
offerings to the Goddess, and it is also used for libations.
Find one you like. Let it fill your emotional and
spiritual womb. May it remind you of your ability
to create and recharge emotionally.

THE BROOM

The broom is to the masculine what the chalice is to the feminine. It is a symbol full of power and intention. Ancient witches were said to put hallucinatory herbs on their brooms and then masturbate with them, which gave them the feeling of flying. Brooms were used to cast circles and in spellwork when witches had to keep their practice private, because brooms, or besoms, were such normal everyday tools. You can use a cinnamon broom to cleanse your space, "sweeping" the air out of the front door. You can also hang one above your door or fireplace.

THE ATHAME

The athame, or ritual knife, is a dagger that might be anything from a few inches to twelve inches long, with a black handle. Among other things, the athame is used in magick to cast (and cut) circles, bless water and draw pentagrams to protect, invoke or banish.

THE WAND

The wand is connected to the Element of Fire in the tarot; it represents inspired action and a connection to intuition and our Higher Self. The wand can be used to cast a circle or to direct energy.

creating an altar

A major suggestion for any new witch is to create an altar. Not only will this intentional act help to make your space more sacred, it will give you a place in which to focus and grow—not to mention work—your magick. We'll be looking again at altars on page 95 as a form of sacred space, but it's never too early to start thinking about creating one of your own.

You'll need: a space where you can house your altar, like a dresser or table, and any objects that correspond to whatever you're trying to honor or manifest (these can include crystals, flowers, photographs, books, candles, talismans and more—see the Tables of Correspondences on pages 274–77 for more ideas).

STEP 1: CLEANSE THE ALTAR

As an altar is a sacred space where energy is consciously worked with, it should be cleansed regularly to keep unwanted and negative vibes out. Before you begin, make sure there's nothing on the space you want to consecrate as part of your altar.

Press your feet into the Earth, take a few deep breaths and connect to the Universe. What is it that your altar is helping you with? Do you want a space to connect you with your life and/or higher purpose? Or do you just want a safe space in which to explore new ideas? Keep that intent in mind as you cleanse the surface of your altar with sage or palo santo. You can also wipe down the surface with Florida water (a citrus-based cologne known for its cleansing properties and smell), rose water or crystal-infused water (quartz and amethyst elixirs would be perfect).

STEP 2: INVITE IN YOUR HIGHER SELF

Once you've physically cleansed your altar, it's time to ask the Universe and your Higher Self for their compassion and blessing. You can also address any beings, deities, angels, masters or saints you work with for their blessing.

STEP 3: DECORATE THAT BABY UP!

Now comes the fun. Time to decorate! You can place candles, crystals, magickal items, talismans and photos on your altar. The colors that correspond to chakras in the chart on page 90 also correspond to color magick and candle magick. You could, for example, create an all-white altar, with white candles, quartz, moonstone and white roses on it for peace. Maybe you want to dedicate an altar to a loved one who's passed away. You can have an altar that serves no greater purpose than just being a working space that looks beautiful. Decorate it in any way you see fit, and, if you wish, search Pinterest, Tumblr and Instagram for inspiration. If it's to be a working altar (where you'll be working spells), remember to leave space for a grimoire and some candles.

If you don't know where to start, pick out one object as a focal point. This could be an old ornate candle, a crystal, a book, a picture of your grandma, an offering like fruit or flowers, a talisman or something else. Add candles, dried flowers, leaves, plants or whatever else you desire.

You can also use your altar as a way to honor your ancestors and guides. Leave them fruit, milk, honey, liquor and sweets as an offering. Write them a poem, and then read it to them every morning. They are listening.

STEP 4: GROUND AND REPEAT

You can cleanse your altar again, once all the objects are on it, or simply ground your energy and enjoy the fruits of your labor! Make an effort to stop by your altar daily. Here are a few ways to do that:

» Light a candle each morning and thank/pray to your guides and ancestors.

» Pull a tarot card each morning and add it on to your altar.

» Charge your clothing for the next day by laying it on your altar and placing crystals on top of the pieces. Charge your keys or wallet by placing green and black stones around them for creativity, abundance and protection.

holidays of the witch

The witch lives by the cycle not only of the Moon but also of the Sun. We acknowledge the Cosmos as these heavenly bodies are reborn, growing and dying each year.

Each month, witches celebrate the full Moon through gatherings known as full Moon esbats, although esbats can be held at other times depending on when a coven chooses to meet up.

Witches celebrate sabbats to mark the passing of the seasons. These include the Equinoxes and the Winter and Summer Solstices, as well as the days falling halfway between these, which are known as cross-quarter days. The sabbats are the high and holy days for the witch, when the atmosphere is charged like electricity for magick, manifestation and reflection. The eight sabbats form what's known as the Wheel of the Year.

We celebrate the sabbats as a way to connect with the Earth and her changing seasons. We celebrate as our ancestors did thousands of years ago—to connect us to that ancient power that comes from living by the cycles of the Sun and Moon.

Each holiday is celebrated with a corresponding altar and ritual. Read through each holiday below a couple of times so you grow familiar with all of them. All of the suggestions can be adapted; get creative if you wish to celebrate with your loved ones or friends. The rituals should feel good to *you*.

The Wheel of the Year is different depending on which hemisphere you live in. This diagram shows the Wheel of the Year for the Northern hemisphere, when summer falls in June and winter in December.

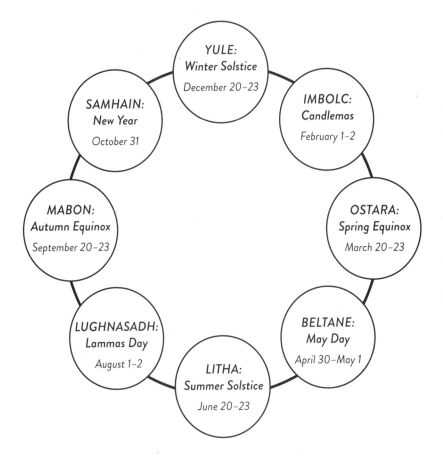

YULE:
Winter Solstice
December 20–23

IMBOLC:
Candlemas
February 1–2

SAMHAIN:
New Year
October 31

OSTARA:
Spring Equinox
March 20–23

MABON:
Autumn Equinox
September 20–23

BELTANE:
May Day
April 30–May 1

LUGHNASADH:
Lammas Day
August 1–2

LITHA:
Summer Solstice
June 20–23

THE MYTH OF THE CHANGING SEASONS*

For witches, the myth of the God and the Goddess represents and mimics the Earth's changing seasons, dying in winter and reborn each spring. There are various manifestations that represent the forces at work. Some choose to honor these archetypes as deities. They include:

The Oak King: God of forest and Earth, the Oak King rules the waxing year and defeats the Holly King at the Winter Solstice. He rules from December (Yule) until June (Summer Solstice, or Midsummer).

The Holly King: A woody version of Santa Claus, the Holly King is the god of the waning year, who defeats the Oak King at Midsummer. He rules from June (Midsummer) to December (Yule).

The Great Mother or Goddess: At Yule, the Goddess gives birth to the Sun God. At Midsummer, she meets her son/consort and they embrace so completely that their love mimics death.

The Sun God: According to the myth that threads through the seasons of the year, the Sun God becomes the lover of the Goddess, thereby fertilizing the Earth and bringing it back to life in summer. At the Autumn Equinox he becomes known as the Lord of the Shadows, in preparation for the darkness of winter.

---

*There are also different individual stories and myths for each of the festivals, which you may like to research further as you develop your craft.

yule: the winter solstice

DECEMBER 20 TO 23

Winter is coming, but really. Yule represents the transition into the season, marking the longest night of the year and the beginning of the waxing year, when the Sun's light starts to increase. The Winter Solstice has been celebrated in some form or other across the world for thousands of years. Stonehenge circle is oriented to frame the Winter Solstice sunset.

The Winter Solstice is a time for us to talk to our shadows. For us to lie in the darkness and talk to anything we've left behind. It's a day when we can honor the hurts we home in our souls and transmute them to lessons and medicine for the coming year. It's an invitation to turn shadows into light.

How to decorate your altar: pine cones; herbs like mistletoe, holly, evergreen, ash bark, thistle; white and silver candles; heirlooms or talismans that connect you to your ancestors; a yule log; the Death tarot card.

Non-ritual ways to celebrate: spend time near a fire; read your tarot; make mulled wine; play outside; buy yourself or loved ones gifts.

Suggested ritual: *a fire ritual to let go of what's no longer serving you*

You'll need: a fireplace, cauldron or fireproof bowl; paper and a pen; herbs like rosemary, rue or cinnamon, palo santo or sage; a lighter.

» Find somewhere safe to light an open flame (like a fireplace or fire pit, or a cauldron or fire-safe bowl).

» Take a ritual bath (see page 181) with salt, rosemary and rue to help ground you and keep you protected.

» Get out of the bath, taking your time to dry off and ground yourself, before getting dressed and asking your angels and guides for assistance and compassion.

» Cast your circle (see "How to Cast a Circle," pages 45–47).

» Write down on a piece of paper whatever it is that you want to let go of in the next six months (a toxic relationship, bad living situation or negative habit, etc.).

» Rip up the paper and place the pieces in the bowl, asking your cosmic team for guidance and messages.

» Light the paper and gaze at the flame, knowing that as this paper burns away, it's releasing your attachment to any old, unhelpful patterns of behavior.

» Sprinkle over the fire protection herbs like rosemary, rue and cinnamon.

» Imagine the energy accumulating from the burning papers as a cone of power, extending from the base of your circle and tapering up over your head. (This is when you're releasing your magick and energy into the Universe where they can do their work.)

» Sense this energy leaving you until you feel settled. Then close the circle.

» Ground and center yourself.

» Toss the cooled ashes to the wind as an offering to the Universe.

imbolc: candlemas

FEBRUARY 1

Imbolc is the first cross-quarter day of the year, a day that falls halfway between the Winter Solstice and Spring Equinox. Imbolc celebrates the approaching return of spring. Just like when the groundhog wakes up and looks for its shadow on this day, Imbolc marks the Earth waking up after the slumber of winter. It celebrates the promise of new life and beginnings. Traditionally Imbolc was a day to celebrate the Celtic goddess Brigid and ask for her protection for the home, crops and livestock.

Imbolc is a time to start making our way up from the shadowy depths of our souls that we explored during Yule. Imbolc is the day when we are allowed to thaw our pains with medicine from the Sun, and grow what we want to as we approach the Spring Equinox and the start of a new cycle.

How to decorate your altar: seeds and plants; cinnamon, daffodil, rosemary or lavender; a spoonful of soil; a Brigid cross or doll; red, white or green candles; poetry, writing and art; white or red flowers; a cauldron filled with dirt to represent the Earth. Tarot cards such as the Three of Wands or the Star.

Non-ritual ways to celebrate: spend time outside; talk to the Sun; journal; write a list of goals and projects to nurture; spend time with a baby; meditate; buy new plants; take a bath or stargaze.

Suggested ritual: *a candle magick ritual for inspiration and abundance*

You'll need: a white taper candle (a chime candle works perfectly for this); white, yellow or pink flowers; rosemary or lavender oil; a chime or bell (optional); and a piece of paper and a pen.

» Cleanse your space with palo santo or sage (see page 18).

» Ring any bells or chimes.

» Ground and center yourself.

» Cast your circle and call in the Elements (see pages 41 and 45).

» Imagine white light surrounding you as you hold your candle.

» You may call upon Brigid/your guides or masters/whichever deity you wish for inspiration and meditate on this feeling.

» Cleanse your pen and candle with sacred smoke.

» On your piece of paper, write down any artistic and creative endeavors that you want to manifest. Fit this into a single short sentence that you can carve into your candle.

» Carve the words into your candle using a pen, toothpick or needle, from the base of the candle up.

» Take your oil and anoint your candle by rubbing from the top to the middle, then the bottom to the middle.

» Set your candle in a holder, placing flowers around it (carefully, so they don't burn).

» Light your candle (as you take note of what the flame looks like).

» Then say:

> "On this sacred Brigid's day, may this candle light the way. May it shine on my creativity that flows as abundantly as the sea."

» Dance, sing or chant to raise the energy.

» At the peak of this activity, imagine the energy accumulating from the base of your circle, tapering up over your head in a cone of power. Then imagine white light shooting from the crown of your head into the Cosmos.

» Let the candle burn if you can, but use a candle snuffer or fan the flame out if you can't let it burn down safely. Never leave a candle burning unattended, use candle holders and keep your candles away from anything flammable. You can also let your candles burn safely in a sink if needed.

» Close the circle.

» Ground your energy.

» You can dispose of the candle wax by burying it or disposing of it carefully at a crossroads or intersection. This way the energy will scatter and "get lost" so it can do its work.

» If necessary, relight the candle and repeat the visualization the next day, letting the candle burn down completely. This shouldn't take more than three days after the initial ritual.

ostara: the spring equinox

MARCH 20 TO 23

Ostara, or the Spring Equinox, marks the first official day of spring, when night and day are of equal length. The return of spring is celebrated all over the world—from Christian Easter to

Jewish Passover to Iranian New Year, known as Nowruz. For witches, the Spring Equinox is known as Ostara, named after the Germanic lunar goddess, an embodiment of the great Goddess who gave birth to the Sun God at the Winter Solstice. As an Equinox, Ostara is a time of balance and equilibrium.

The Spring Equinox is a reminder that it's time to celebrate and plant seeds, both metaphorically and physically, for what we want to bring to bloom in the upcoming season. It's also a time when we honor all the things we've achieved since the Winter Solstice. It's time to bloom, breathe, create, procreate and reap the sweetness of what we've manifested, as we're brought even closer to the light.

How to decorate your altar: any flowers (especially warm colors); black and white candles; seeds, citrus, fruits, pomegranates, honey; citrine, clear quartz, aventurine; an offering of milk or honey for the faeries. Tarot cards such as the High Priestess and Nine of Cups may also adorn your altar.

Non-ritual ways to celebrate: plant flowers or garden; take a walk in the Sun and talk to the trees; spring clean your home and donate old clothing to charity; collect flowers and press them in a vintage frame; enjoy a picnic in a field; swim or lie outside naked with the Sun kissing your skin.

Suggested ritual: *a plant meditation for growth and spiritual connection*

You'll need: a potted plant like a violet or ivy—something to which you feel connected and that can live in your sacred space.

» Cleanse your space with palo santo, sage or cedar.

» Ground and center yourself.

» Cast your circle.

» Hold your plant in your hand, thinking of how she connects you to the Universe. May you tend to her as you tend to your inner world. May she remind you that there's always balance in the chaos.

» If you're repotting your own plant, this is the time to do so.

» Next, take a seat and place your plant in front of you. Imagine the energy of this plant sitting at your heart, her roots extending down through your legs into the Earth. Her vines and leaves are growing out through your arms and through the top of your head, connecting back to the Earth.

» What does the energy of your plant feel like? What does she remind you of? Do you feel a connection to a faery? Record any thoughts, feelings or visions in your grimoire.

» Close the circle.

» Ground your energy.

» Connect with this energy whenever you tend to the plant. Tell your plant sweet and loving things. Ask it for guidance. Build a relationship with the spirit of the plant and listen to it!

beltane: may day

APRIL 30 TO MAY 1

May Day, which takes place on May Day eve and May 1, is the second cross-quarter day of the year, falling between the Spring Equinox and the Summer Solstice. The maypole is probably the most famous image of this holiday of fire and fertility, which marks the approach of summer and all the sensuality that the returning Sun brings with it. Beltane represents sacred sexuality, and the eternal cycle of sacrifice and rebirth needed for the continuation of life. At Beltane, the ancient Celts honored Bel, the god of light and fire who represents the deity that impregnates the Great Mother. The Celts would celebrate by lighting bel-fires, or bonfires, to mark the return of light to the world, a practice that is continued today.

May Day is a day to reassess how and why we light our flame. What turns your heart on? How about your body and soul? What is it that you'd like to continue manifesting this season? This is a day for passion, growth and love of any and all kinds.

How to decorate your altar: flowers of all kinds; flower crowns and colorful ribbons; sprigs of rosemary, motherwort and marigold; the Lovers tarot card.

Non-ritual ways to celebrate: spend time outside; having a bonfire; making (and wearing) a flower crown; leaving offerings of milk, honey or fruit for the faeries; making love; divination; picking flowers or fruit.

Suggested ritual: *a rose-quartz self-love ritual*

You'll need: a piece of selenite (one that's not too rough on your skin); a smooth piece of rose quartz; a mirror, flowers, and rose oil or massage oil.

» Cleanse your space with palo santo or sage.

» Put a vase of roses or flowers on your altar, and slip into something that makes you feel sexy and empowered.

» Ground and center yourself.

» Cast a circle.

» Find a comfortable seat.

» Cleanse your aura with the selenite, starting at the crown of your head and then moving the crystal around your neck, arms, palms, heart, torso, legs and soles of the feet.

» Place your mirror in front of you, putting some oil on your legs.

» Use your rose quartz to start massaging the bottom of your feet, moving up each leg.

» Imagine a shining golden light from the crystal infusing your flesh.

» Give yourself compliments, saying what you like about each part of your body. (There's always something, even if it's just "I love how my legs carry me through my day without pain" or "I'm so thankful for this heart that stays open!")

» Move up your legs, adding oil as needed, to your pelvic bones and torso, up your arms, throat and over the third eye (a spiritual gateway located in the forehead, just above and between the eyebrows), toward the crown of your head. End back down at your heart. You should feel like you're in a warm cocoon of golden light.

» When you feel a slight vibration or warmth, or simply feel ready, say:

"I bless this temple with quartz of rose, I bless this open heart as an open door."

» Imagine your heart as the most beautiful door you've ever seen, opening to the Universe to receive all the love and offerings she has in store for you.

» Then say:

> "*May this love be ever-present; may I savor this connection.*"

» Take this time to focus on all the things that make you happy and that you love about yourself.

» As your energy rises, imagine a cone of power extending from the base of your circle to the top of your head into the Universe in a stream of golden light.

» Release your intention into the Cosmos, knowing that an abundance of love is waiting for you.

» Close the circle and ground your energy.

» Record your experience in your grimoire.

litha: the summer solstice or midsummer

JUNE 20 TO 23

Lap it up, baby! It's summer! Time to let go of the winter blues and step into your most beautiful, expansive self. Midsummer is the longest day of the year and the shortest night. It's also the beginning of the waning season. Today is the energetic climax of the year, when the Sun is at his peak. It's time to celebrate all the love we've given, all the ass we've kicked, all the work we've put in and all we've accomplished in the past six months.

Midsummer is when the Cosmos is holding and supporting us, when we're allowed to release anything we've been keeping in. What creative venture is waiting to burst forth? What can you continue to nurture into the next season?

How to decorate your altar: roses and other summer flowers; red, gold or orange candles; a chalice or cauldron filled with water; bundles of red and white heather; oak and holly leaves; and the Sun tarot card.

Non-ritual ways to celebrate: make a bonfire; swim in the ocean or a pool; take a walk in the park and leave an offering for the faeries; drink wine in a field with lovers or friends; buy yourself some flowers; wear sunny, golden colors; make love and enjoy the energetic peak of the year.

Suggested ritual: *a rose petal spell and offering for sweet manifestations*

You'll need: a rose for each person taking part; a cauldron or bowl; oil with properties that relate to what you're manifesting (if you choose); herbs such as lavender, St. John's wort, sage, mint (which are all linked to this time of year); crystals like carnelian, clear quartz, citrine, tiger's eye and garnet; a pen (gold or silver ink would be best, but black will still work).

» Find a space where you can remain undisturbed.

» Ground yourself.

» Cast a circle.

» Settle yourself down in the center of your circle with your roses and crystals.

» Then say:

> *"On this Summer Solstice day, these roses listen and hear my prayers. May they manifest with ease and grace, all while working in my highest favor."*

» State an intention as you pick a petal from the rose. You can use the same intention on multiple petals, picking them individually or as a bunch, dropping each of them into the cauldron or bowl.

» If you are performing this ritual with others, take turns, with each of you holding the space as the other declares his or her intention.

» If you wish, write what you want to manifest on the petals.

» Continue until your roses hold no more petals.

» Now make an offering of your herbs and oils, adding these to the cauldron or bowl. The flowers are beings who hear you: know that they are listening, and feel what it will be like when you manifest your intentions.

» Imagine the energy accumulating from the ritual you've just completed, then rising in the form of a cone of power, extending from the base of your circle and tapering up over your head. This is when you're releasing your magick and energy into the Universe so it can do its work.

» Feel this energy leaving you until you feel settled.

» Close the circle.

» Ground your power.

» Take the rose petals somewhere outside. If there is a natural body of water near you, this would be ideal. Cast the petals to the wind or water, thanking them for their work and returning them to the Earth as an offering. You can also make oil from the roses, or sew them into a pink sachet with rosemary and tuck it into your pillow.

lughnasadh or lammas day

AUGUST 1

Lughnasadh, named after the Celtic Sun god Lugh, is a cross-quarter day and the first of the three harvest holidays, marking the beginning of the harvest season. The day is celebrated with feasting, games and song. It's when we welcome in the impending darkness on an energetic level. Our spirits begin to shift and prepare for autumn: something wicked this way comes!

What needs more nourishment? How about less? Lammas allows us to see how our goals from Midsummer are holding up, and it offers us the opportunity to prepare ourselves for the coming season; physically, emotionally and spiritually.

How to decorate your altar: grains; poppies; bilberries; wheat and other seasonal pickings; candles in autumn colors like gold, brown and burgundy; dark red and orange stones like citrine, carnelian, tiger's eye and amber; the Sun tarot card.

Non-ritual ways to celebrate: bake fresh bread; pick crops or make a list of that which you intend to harvest, both spiritually and mentally, keeping this list where you can see it; spend time nurturing yourself or your loved ones; write in your journal; read the tarot; and take time to give thanks for the bounty ahead.

Suggested ritual: *a spell to recalibrate and nurture new beginnings*

You'll need: a pen and paper; your grimoire; a fireproof bowl or cauldron; citrus oils or Florida water; sage, palo santo or cedar; and a plant if you have one.

» Cleanse your space with the sacred smoke of sage, palo santo or cedar.

» Ground and center yourself, connecting to the energy of the Earth.

» Cast your circle.

» Fold your paper in half, thinking about the next two months and the start of autumn.

» On the right side of the paper, write down what nourishes you.

» On the left, write down what no longer nourishes you.

» Be as specific as you can, taking inventory of what feeds your energy and what depletes it.

» Rip the two sections apart.

» Take a look at what's depleting you energetically. In your grimoire, write down five ways you can shift these things so they feed you, or five new ways to find nourishment.

» Tear up the half of the paper listing what's depleting you and burn it.

» You can anoint the list of what's nourishing you by rubbing the oil or Florida water on it in the form of an invoking pentagram (starting from the top down to the bottom left, up to the right, to the left, down to the bottom right and then up to the top).

» When you feel ready, fold this half of the paper up. You can either leave it under your plant or on your altar until the next full Moon, or bury it somewhere outside once this ritual is complete.

» Close your eyes and feel what it would be like to be supported, nourished and cared for in all your ventures.

» Raise energy by chanting, dancing, singing or masturbating.

» At the climax, imagine a cone of power extending from the boundaries of your circle up through the crown of your head into the Universe: this is your declaration of nourishment and health. Know it's promised.

» Close your circle.

» Ground your energy.

On the next full Moon, take stock and check in to see how fulfilled and nourished you feel, and how you can let go of whatever's keeping you from feeling supported.

mabon: the autumn equinox

SEPTEMBER 20 TO 23

Everyone knows what it feels like when autumn arrives. The air hangs heavier, the veil feels murkier, there's something that shifts. This officially begins on Mabon, the first day of autumn, when night and day are of equal length. Autumn is a time of balance, a theme played out by the Sun, which enters the sign of Libra, the scales. Mabon is when the harvest is completed and we look forward at the impending winter as a time of death, rebirth and transformation. It's a day of being grateful and giving thanks.

The Autumn Equinox is a time to see the abundance set before us so we can enter the darkness and await the transformation that's promised there. The Autumn Equinox is when we allow ourselves to begin to transform into our fullest selves. This is like the witch's Thanksgiving Day, when we say thank you to the Universe for all of her abundance.

How to decorate your altar: squash and gourds; leaves; acorns, seeds, nuts and pine cones; feathers; anything that makes you feel rich and grounded. An ear of corn was said to be at the center of the Eleusinian mysteries, and this may be an addition to your altar if it calls to you. The Ten of Pentacles card may find its way onto your altar as well.

Non-ritual ways to celebrate: make some apple cider; spend a bit of time in a graveyard; watch a scary movie and eat your favorite comfort food; spend time collecting beautiful leaves and arrange them in a vintage frame; take a walk in the park, thanking the trees and flowers for their gifts; make a list of everything you're grateful for—and thank the Universe for it.

Suggested ritual: *an apple and element ritual for guidance and protection*

This ritual is to prepare for the coming winter, to remind us that we are supported even in the darkest time of year.

You'll need: a knife, an apple (or a pomegranate or citrus fruit if you're allergic to apples) and a white tea light candle.

» Cleanse your space with sage and a cinnamon broom if you have one.

» Ground yourself.

» Cast your circle.

» Call in the energy of gratitude and meditate on the idea of abundance. Feel this white light spread throughout your chest and your being.

» Cut the apple in half, width-wise. When it's cut, you'll see the seeds resemble the shape of a star.

» Carve out a hole on one side big enough for your white tea light.

» Place the candle in the apple and say:

"Even at the winter hour, I shall always find my power. May I always see my path, and know abundance as a fact."

» Light the candle, asking any guardian angels and deities to bless the light as you move toward winter. This white candle represents the internal guidance and light that you always have in you.

» Take the other half of the apple.

» Eat one bite and say:

"Element of Earth, may I always feel your protection."

» Eat another bite and say:

"Element of Air, may I always feel your guidance."

» Eat another bite and say:

"Element of Fire, may I always feel your passion."

» Eat another bite and say:

"Element of Water, may I always feel your support."

» Eat one more bite, or the rest of the piece, and say:

"Element of Spirit, may I feel the cosmic thread connecting me to you.

May I see your light whenever I need it. So mote it be."

- » Visualize a white light surrounding you. Sit with this.

- » Release this energy as a cone of power, extending from the base of your circle and tapering up over your head. This is when you're releasing your magick and energy into the Universe so it can do its work.

- » Feel this energy leaving you until you feel settled.

- » Close the circle and ground yourself.

- » Once the tea light has finished burning, bury or throw the apple away at a crossroads or intersection.

samhain: the witch's new year

OCTOBER 31

IT'S THE NEW YEAR! AND IT'S HALLOWEEN! If there's one day you can really let your inner freaky witch out, it's on Samhain. Also known as the witch's New Year, Samhain celebrates all we've accomplished and allows us to do so alongside those who have made it happen: our ancestors. The veil that separates us from them is like a curtain, and we're able to peek behind it much more easily now than at any other time of year.

Honoring our ancestors, our roots, our families and ourselves is an overarching theme of Samhain, when we're encouraged to engage with the Other Side. Halloween feels different from the other sabbats—and that's because it is! May we use the witch's New Year to recharge and reset ourselves.

How to decorate your altar: roses and brightly colored flowers; skulls; seasonal decorations like squash, gourds, acorns and seeds; candles in autumn colors such as black, deep red and orange; heirlooms and talismans that connect you to your ancestors; any offerings to icons and loved ones on the Other Side; Death and the Moon tarot cards are also appropriate.

Non-ritual ways to celebrate: go trick-or-treating; have a midnight picnic in a cemetery; write a letter to your deceased loved ones and then burn it; leave an offering of mulled wine for your ancestors; talk to the Moon and enjoy the night.

Suggested ritual: *an ancestral blessing spell for a sweet New Year*

You'll need: a pomegranate (if you're allergic, use an apple instead); a pen and your grimoire; pictures of any deceased relatives or loved ones, icons or guides, etc., on your altar; an athame or wand; a bowl and a black tea candle.

» Cleanse, cleanse and cleanse your space. This is the most important and energetically charged time of the year and you want to make sure your space feels safe and inviting.

» Ground and center yourself, asking to connect with the wisdom and spirit of your ancestors.

» Cast a circle, and as you finish inviting in the Elements, invite your ancestors to join you as well.

WE CELEBRATE
TO CONNECT WITH
THE EARTH AND
THE CHANGING
SEASONS AS OUR
ANCESTORS DID
THOUSANDS OF
YEARS AGO.

» Say:

"As we gather on this day, we're reminded of how thin the veil hangs. Ancestors and guides, I ask for your compassion, for your love and your direction. Join me now at this Samhain celebration, as we reflect on this past year and give thanks for its manifestations."

» Dividing in half a page in your grimoire, write a list of "thorns" and "roses" for the year, taking note of all the good and the bad, and seeing how they balance out.

» Once completed, move to your altar.

» Recite each "rose" to your ancestors, eating a pomegranate seed for each one (or taking a bite of apple). Imagine each pomegranate seed manifesting more of every good thing.

» When you're done with listing your "roses," use your athame or wand to draw the sign of the invoking pentagram above the altar and say:

"This next year, may I see only roses in front of me."

» Follow the same steps for your "thorns," except instead of eating a pomegranate seed for each one, place the seeds in the bowl as an offering to your ancestors.

» Draw the banishing pentagram above your altar and say:

"May I see these thorns as opportunities. May my ancestors show me the way to light, love and wisdom even on the darkest days."

» Light your black candle, take five deep breaths and gaze into the light.

» Soften your focus and notice any feelings or images you see in the flame. Is anyone coming to mind? Do you sense any messages from loved ones? If you can, let the candle burn all the way down.

» Thank your ancestors, offering them the pomegranate seeds.

» Once you feel ready, you can dismiss your ancestors, allowing them to return to the spirit realm while saying something like:

"Ancestors, I feel your spirits and I thank you for hearing and honoring my call. May I always remember your wisdom and presence. I know you're always with me. I thank you for coming to this ritual and dismiss you. Blessed be."

» Close the circle.

» Ground and center yourself, recording anything you have observed or experienced in your grimoire.

» If some of the candle is left, let it burn down safely over the next three days. After three days, you can leave your pomegranate seeds outside as an offering to the natural world.

CHAPTER TWO

everything is energy

So, Wild One, now you know that the Universe is both chaotic and peaceful, and that the dual nature found in her is also found in you. That as she turns, so you turn. That to cast spells, the most important thing to keep in mind is your intention and any actions necessary to manifest it. You've discovered the Witch's Laws that turn chaos into creation, spells into magick and magick into reality. Now it's time to learn about yourself; about the more subtle aspect of your being that you've been dancing with your whole life, perhaps unknowingly.

Have you ever felt something in the pit of your stomach—like sensing that something's wrong—only to be proven right later on? Have you ever felt the energy in a room tense up when a stranger steps into your space? Maybe you had a feeling you shouldn't have gone to something, only to go and have it be a total disaster. I get it all the time and it's completely normal. It's called intuition, baby!

Intuition works with the subtle body (aka our energetic body) as a messenger for that which we feel but can't necessarily see. Our bodies are surrounded by energy fields; while radiation and electromagnetic fields can be traced, these energy fields cannot. Instead, they're perceived through their effects. The aura is the most intimate part of our energetic field, like a level of our personal universe that affects us the most. The aura, along with other parts of our subtle body, receives and sends information to the rest of the body like an antenna.

the aura

The aura is an egg-shaped field of electromagnetic energy that surrounds us. Most of us can't see it unless it's captured by an aura photograph, but many of us can feel it. Think of your aura as being like your very own personal cloud that tells the world how you're feeling energetically, emotionally, physically and spiritually. You've probably been around someone who makes you feel vibrant and loved just from their presence; this is an aura in action!

Our aura connects us to different planes of energy—including physical and ethereal levels. It also connects us to our chakras, the energy centers that sit along our spine. The aura is only one aspect of our personal energetic field, but it's the one we're most intimate with. The aura is actually divided into seven levels, moving a layer at a time from the physical to the divine and ethereal (just like the layers of the Universe itself), with each layer or level corresponding to a different chakra.

When we're healthy, our aura is said to extend far around us. When our bodies, minds or spirits are sick or out of whack, however, our aura shrinks and its colors are less vibrant. You know how sometimes you can feel someone's negativity? Not that they're necessarily a bad person, but like they're just carrying around a fog of negativity with them? Well, dear ones, that's what I'd describe as someone with a murky aura.

A healthy aura, to those who can see it, resembles a bright and clear cloud of a certain color.

Aura Color	When in balance	When out of balance
Red	Passionate, energetic, sexual and powerful.	Anger, anxiety, obsession and nervousness.
Pink	Loving, tender, sensual, caring and romantic.	Immature, dishonest.
Orange	Confident, creative, intelligent, detail-oriented and artistic.	Stressed out, overwhelmed, overworked and addicted.
Yellow	Awakening, inspiration, easy-going and optimistic.	Fear, straining, stress, overwhelmed and overworked.
Green	Healing, loving, communicative and community-oriented.	Jealous, envious, insecure, low self-esteem and victimized.
Blue	Calm, reserved, emotional, intuitive, spiritual, feeling and sensitive.	Fear of self-expression, fear of honesty and empathic without controlling it.
Indigo	Psychic, visual, honest, aware and connected to Higher Self.	Not grounded, giving to others too much and fear of honesty.
Violet	Most sensitive color, wise, intuitive, magick and futuristic.	Ungrounded and not enough work in the physical.
White	New energy, the purest form of light, angelic, new life and new energy.	Dedicating too much time in the spiritual and not grounded enough in the physical.
Black	There are no positives for having an aura this dark; intense healing is needed.	Long-term lack of forgiveness, past-life issues, grief and overwhelming negativity.

Our auras reflect imbalances in ourselves. To cleanse your aura, you can smudge it with sage, palo santo or selenite. Try sitting in the grass, and imagining a green light surrounding you. Salt baths help to ground and clear our spirits, and are useful if you're feeling anxious, overwhelmed or like you've picked up someone else's energy. As mentioned, since salt is a small crystal, it helps to absorb excess energy, as well as ground our own energy. Salt baths are a potent way of doing this. You can also meditate with a specific color if you need more of the qualities associated with it in your life. For example, if you want to work on being more creative, you can imagine yourself being surrounded by orange light. You can also practice the chakra meditation in the following section.

the chakras

The word "chakra" means "wheel of light" in Sanskrit. The chakras are energy centers located along the spine, with each one corresponding to a different purpose. Although the chakras are originally a Hindu principle, different variations of the system are found throughout the world. There are actually more energy centers than we can count in the human body, but the seven main chakras are the most universally recognized. The chakras are the energy transformers of the body, shifting the vibration of energy from high to low, or vice versa. They are the collectors and transmitters of the energetic body, and are said to be located at the main branches of our nervous system. Just like our immune system keeps us healthy, our chakra system looks after the well-being of our subtle energies and spiritual bodies.

The chakras deal with kundalini, or the life energy that is said to coil at the base of our spine like a serpent. This kundalini energy is associated with the Hindu goddess Shakti, who represents the eternal supreme consciousness. As we awaken our consciousness, the kundalini moves up the chakras along the spine, eventually reaching the last chakra at the top of our head, where the Hindu god Shiva—infinite supreme consciousness—resides. Once the two energies merge, we are "awakened" and freed from the karmic cycles of death and rebirth, and we are said to hold supreme consciousness.

A CHAKRA MEDITATION

This simple meditation will help you align and balance your chakras and aura. Start by imagining a ball of glowing red light at the base of your spine—at your root chakra. This red glowing ball stays there as you breathe into it for a few deep breaths. Then it moves up to your sacral chakra, turning orange along the way. Breathe into this before it moves up to your solar plexus chakra and turns yellow. Do this with each chakra, imagining the light changing to the corresponding color as it moves upward.

When it gets to the crown of your head, imagine it being here for a few breaths before it then starts to move back down your spine, going from white to violet to blue, all the way down.

You can also imagine flowers opening at each chakra in the corresponding colors, blooming as you move up and folding back in as you move down your body. Use the same flowers in each of your chakra meditations, but remember to close your chakras if you open them. This will help you stay balanced.

Chakra	Color	Mantra	Balanced
Muladhara: root chakra. Located at the base of the spine.	Red	*Lam*	Perseverance, passionate about life and grounded. When this chakra is in balance, we feel like we have all the necessities (food, water, shelter) that allow us to live and create safely.
Svadhishthana: sacral chakra. Located between navel and genitals.	Orange	*Vam*	Creative, abundant and sexually empowered; the ability to create and nurture love and sweetness. When this chakra is balanced we can express ourselves in unique and creative ways.
Manipura: third chakra. Located at the solar plexus.	Yellow	*Ram*	Confident, assured, powerful, energetic—like the flame in your soul is alive and healthy. (This chakra is like the Sun!) Powerful, goal-oriented, motivated and having a strong sense of purpose.
Anahata: fourth chakra. Located at the heart.	Green	*Ram*	Love, compassion, forgiveness, empathy, receptiveness and awareness. The heart chakra is where the physical and spiritual meet. Living with an open heart chakra means living with an open heart: receiving and giving love and positive affirmation.
Vishuddha: fifth chakra. Located at the throat.	Blue	*Ham*	Communication, spiritual connection to our guides and ancestors and soul. The throat chakra guides our ability to speak our truth to the world. It also connects the physical body (linked to the previous four chakras) with the subtle body (connected with the top two chakras). This chakra allows us to connect to our highest truth and to our dreams.

Imbalanced	To Balance
Struggling for balance and stability. Suffering from anxiety, fear and nightmares.	Meditate. Work with red gemstones (like garnet, red jasper, bloodstone). Trust in the Universe. Write letters to your guides and deities, and burn them.
Unhealthy sex life and frustrated creatively; scared of stepping into your own unique personality. Blocked from joy and creative expression.	Play! Do something creative to ignite your Inner Child. Get in touch with your emotions by journaling, meditating, having sex or making self-love.
Anger-management issues, low self-esteem and feeling lost. Being overbearing or overly authoritative.	Try something new. Work with yellow gems like topaz and tiger's eye. Place your hand over your solar plexus and ask it questions about possible outcomes, listening to what "feels" right. Wear yellow, meditate.
Grief, anger, sadness, jealousy, hatred, betrayal. Victimization and unhealthy emotional boundaries. Bitterness at love, sadness, hurt. No empathy or sympathy for other people.	Work with green stones like jade and emerald, as well as rose quartz. Smile at strangers, love yourself, tell family and loved ones the things you like about them. Write down all your grudges, burn them and bury the ashes. Make a list of positive affirmations to say to yourself.
Fear of not being accepted, fear of embodying your voice, fear of judgment. Not being able to communicate or say what we need, or what we mean.	Chanting, singing, humming and practicing *pranayama* (breathing techniques). Work with blue stones like lapis lazuli, turquoise and sapphire. Writing, talking to a professional, putting your voice and words out there.

Chakra	Color	Mantra	Balanced
Ajna: sixth chakra. Located at the third eye.	Violet	*Om*	Inner sight, higher consciousness, awareness and melting of the distinction between "I" and "you" into "One." Intuition, connection to the Higher Self and "seeing" things with our third eye. Our psychic and extrasensory powers reside here.
Sahasrara: seventh chakra. Located at the crown of the head.	White	None	Connection to ourselves, the Universe and every being on this planet. Unconditional love and awareness, and breaking free of karmic cycles. Being able to live in the present. Compassion, kindness and bliss. Forgiveness and selflessness.

Imbalanced	To Balance
Difficulty accessing intuition or trusting our inner voice. Judgmental, dismissive, unaware of the workings of our inner world. Suffering from dizziness, headaches, sadness, disconnection from reality and anxiety.	Meditation, visualization, listening to your intuition. Ritual, magick, dance, trance work. Working with amethyst, lapis lazuli and azurite. Practicing *pranayama*.
Sadness, depression, lack of empathy, confusion, victimization, not connecting to others or to the natural world. Sensitivity to light and sound. Not being truly present.	Prayer, meditation, silence. Spiritual practices and yoga. Ritual and ceremony. Choose love, and work on your ego. Work with amethyst and clear crystals like angel aura quartz and clear quartz.

sacred
space

I think it's impossible to enter a beautiful place of worship and not *feel* something. After all, in the end, we're all praying to the same thing, right? I like to think that each temple and church honors divinity in its own way, creating a sacred space it thinks its god or goddess would adore; and this shows in the way these spaces are decorated. Usually, they're maintained and cleansed in a certain way. Both Hinduism and Catholicism, for example, rely on the smoke of sacred herbs and incense. Some spiritual seekers use holy water and Florida water to cleanse surfaces, or some places let sunlight pour into the space to clear the energy.

Most of us don't live in a church or temple, but that doesn't mean we can't create our own sacred space as a way to ground, honor and manifest our desires. If you take the time to physically clean your home, why wouldn't you take the time to clean it energetically as well? As with opening and carefully closing the chakras, a sacred space needs to be maintained and protected. Our energy fields are kind of like batteries: they need to be recharged. When we take time to find solitude, having a space that supports and charges us is vital. If you're lucky enough to have a space of your own, utilize it! Make it your temple.

Having a sacred space means creating an energetic environment that supports your work as a witch. For example, I would consider my room my sacred space. I use herbs like sage and palo santo to cleanse it multiple times a week (see Smudging on pages 18–20). I love to do this on Sunday, after I've cleaned and wiped down surfaces with Florida water and rose water. I do most of my spells, readings, crying, wishing, hoping and whatever else in my room. I have flowers everywhere and am very intentional about who or what I let in.

Redirecting the energy of a space, cleansing it with smoke and decorating it with correspondences like crystals, herbs and flowers are all good ways to start creating a sacred space. If you feel drawn to creating even more harmony in your space, perhaps learn about feng shui, which is the Chinese philosophy of creating harmony with your environment by mapping how your space corresponds to different aspects of your life.

You can dedicate your space to your craft if you wish, or you can simply cleanse it intentionally. Perhaps you'll create a simple weekly ritual as well. Here are a few more ways to do this:

» Sprinkle salt in the corners to absorb excess energy.

» Place selenite in the space.

» Charge a quartz crystal and place it at the entrance (see pages 234–35 for how to charge a crystal).

» Diffuse essential oils.

» Create and dedicate an altar (see pages 54–56).

» Wipe down surfaces with Florida water, crystal-infused water (water that has, or had, crystals steeped in it, thereby imparting the stones' properties to it) or rose water.

» Use a cinnamon broom to sweep energy out of your space to clear it.

You could create a cleaning ritual during which you ask blessings from your guides as you clean your space. In any event, give thanks for your space as you clean, while incorporating any or all of the above suggestions into your routine.

maintaining your altar

An altar is a gathering of sacred objects, talismans, crystals, flowers and anything else that serves to connect us with our intent. In Chapter 1, we looked at how to create one, and I explained how your altar should feel personal to you.

I have candles, cards, oils, crystals, talismans, icons and more grouped on my altar, with a separate self-care altar next to it. You'll probably have an everyday altar to which you can add things as the seasons shift and the holidays come and go. You may also have an altar you maintain for a certain amount of time (such as during the separate Moon cycles). You may have one to mourn, one to celebrate and one to manifest. Like anything else in the craft, there are no hard and fast rules. The most important piece of the puzzle is how things feel to you—and they should always feel absolutely divine.

For a witch, an altar not only serves as a focal point for energy and worship, it also serves as a place for magick to take place. Although you can include separate areas in your sacred space for performing different things like candle spells and tarot readings, having a working altar is highly recommended. Having a fixed space for your energy work will only make your altar and magick stronger, helping you form a strong relationship with your space.

As we saw in Chapter 1, creating an altar isn't hard, thankfully! All you need is a flat space where you can do your magickal work and light candles safely. Today, I use the top of my dresser, but when I was in a college dorm, my altar was on my bookshelf. And, if you're not able to have a permanent altar, you can use a box (a wooden one would be the best but I've used plastic) and store your magickal items, an altar cloth and some sage in it when it's not in use. This way you can set up your altar for rituals and magick work whenever you need to.

HOW TO SET UP PROTECTIVE BOUNDARIES AROUND YOUR SACRED SPACE

By setting up protective boundaries around your sacred space, and by creating a protective auric field that you can use whenever you need to, you'll be able to practice your craft in the equivalent of a safe place.

Perform this ritual under a new or waning Moon.

You'll need: a quiet space; four black candles and one white candle (if your space permits it); an athame (or wand); sage or cobalt; sea salt; and black crystals like tourmaline or onyx (to absorb and repel negative energy, respectively). You'll also want to know which way is North.

Step 1: Ground.

The first step in any spell or ritual is to get your energy settled. As this specific ritual is a way to clear, cleanse and protect your sacred space as well as your auric field, you'll want to perform it in the actual space that you want to protect. Turn off all your electronics, make sure you can be alone and uninterrupted and then ground yourself (see page 29–30).

Step 2: Cleanse.

Light some palo santo, sage or cobalt, and walk around your space, asking your guides, masters and/or the Universe to banish anything that's not working in your highest favor. Move intentionally around your room, making sure to cleanse the corners. Once you've hit every area of the room, sprinkle salt in each corner. This works to help absorb excess energy.

Step 3: Cast the circle.

Locate and then face in the direction of North. Cast your circle (see pages 45–47), moving clockwise, asking for protection, guidance and compassion. Imagine an orb of protection holding you.

Step 4: Call in the Elements for protection.

You'll be lighting candles for each direction, starting in the North. Place a black candle between your feet. Say something like the following:

"This is a sacred space, and only that which serves and fulfills my highest calling and mission is welcome. With the blessing of the [North] and Element of the [Earth] guiding and protecting me."

Cast the sign of the banishing pentagram with your athame. (Start at the bottom left corner, moving to the top, back down to the right, up to the left, straight across to the right and then back down to the left.) Then say:

"I banish any entities, energies, beings or feelings that are not working in my highest favor."

Light the black candle (if you can't light candles, place a tourmaline in each direction). Move clockwise and repeat this for each of the remaining directions of the compass (East/Air, South/Fire, West/Water), drawing the pentagram and lighting a candle at the furthermost point of that direction in the circle.

Step 5: The mirrored orb of protection.

Once you've lit all the candles and called on the Elements for protection, move back to the center of your circle and face the North. Draw the banishing pentagram once again. Say:

"This is a space of sacred devotion. This is a circle of deep protection. Each Element I bid you to hear my calling, protect me from anything that could harm me. I banish, I banish, I banish thee, energy and entities of negativity. So it is, so it shall be, by the power of the Universe and through me."

Draw the banishing pentagram one last time, imagining the blade leaving a silver pentacle and moving forward like a lock of protection and security in an iron door before you.

Sit down in a comfortable position and light the white candle in front of you. Close your eyes and take a few deep breaths to slow your mind. Once you feel grounded, imagine a silver orb around you. It is mirrored and surrounds your space, reflecting everything around it. This is your orb of protection; whenever you need it, it's available to you. Only that which serves your highest good, highest favor or Higher Self can get past the mirrors. That which aims to hurt or harm you is reflected back to the sender. Hold this, feel it and thank it.

Step 6: Release.

Once you're ready, dismiss the Elements by walking counterclockwise round the circle and thanking them for their protection. Say, for example:

> "(West), Element of (Water), I thank you for your protection and dismiss you from this ritual. Blessed be."

If you can't let your candles burn all the way down, use a fan or candle snuffer to put them out.

Step 7: Close the circle.

Walk counterclockwise, closing the circle. Say:

> "The circle is open, may it never be broken."

Step 8: Protect and ground your energy.

Place a black stone like onyx or tourmaline at the entrance to your sacred space. Ground your energy by pressing your forehead into the floor and imagine energy returning to the core of the Earth. Give thanks to the Universe for the blessing of her protection. You can bury the remaining candle wax at a crossroads or dispose of it at an intersection. Walk away from it and don't look back when you do.

CHAPTER THREE

divine
the signs:
the tarot

Are you ready to divine the signs? Thanks to the help of the tarot, you can get to know yourself and whoever's cards you're reading in a meaningful way. The tarot is a fortune-telling system that originated in the fifteenth century, most likely in the form of a card game in Italy. Though its true origins are still unknown for certain, the card game eventually became the divination system that most of us are familiar with today.

The tarot consists of a seventy-eight-card deck that's divided into two parts, the Major Arcana and the Minor Arcana, with the word "arcana" coming from the Latin *arcanum*, meaning a secret or mystery. The twenty-two cards of the Major Arcana represent major changes and events, as well as the evolution of humanity itself from the material and physical planes to the spiritual realm; the cards in it, such as Death, the Tower and the Moon, hold more significance in a reading than those in the Minor Arcana because they represent greater transformations. The Minor Arcana represent our day-to-day life and those situations we might face multiple times. This Arcana includes four suits: Cups, Pentacles, Wands and Swords, with four court cards in each suit. Classically, these are the Page, Knight, Queen and King. The court cards represent specific people or archetypal energies.

The tarot doesn't tell our fortune in the way that we might be accustomed to thinking. Instead, the cards act as a map to parts of our unconscious selves that we may be unaware of. They're like mirrors, picking up our energy in a reading and reflecting it back to us.

Instead of showing us something that's set in stone, the tarot offers new ways for us to see a situation, giving us insight and perspective.

The tarot is only one form of divination, and there are other forms of card divination systems out there, such as oracle cards, which are left to the interpretation of the artist and author. However, while the tarot has a set structure, oracle cards do not.

choosing a deck

Although there's a myth that you have to be gifted your first tarot deck, there are many people—myself included—who would dispute this. Having a connection with your deck is vital; there's nothing wrong with choosing your own deck to ensure that you work with cards that you feel connected to.

The most important thing when shopping for a deck is to find one that speaks to you. It should spark your soul! Search online or go into your local metaphysical store to find something that feels right. The most common tarot deck is the Rider-Waite deck, but there are plenty of variations on this, as well as a whole slew of original and indie decks. There's a tarot renaissance going on right now, so there's something for everyone. Scour the internet until you find something you connect with and go from there.

the major arcana

The Major Arcana represent the pivotal moments in our lives, where big changes manifest and major decisions are made. They represent the journeys we take to learn about ourselves on a deep, spiritual level. When these cards show up, pay attention: they signal people, situations and opportunities that we want to take note of. As a numbered sequence, the cards in the Major Arcana represent stages in the spiritual development of humankind. This means that not only do they describe an individual's personal journey, they connect us with spirit, soul and the Universe.

Card	Keywords	Meaning	Reversed Meaning
0: The Fool	Journey, opportunity, adventure, naïveté, freedom, experience and uniqueness.	The beginning of a new venture. Being a little naïve in an optimistic way and starting a journey with complete faith.	Reevaluate and make sure you're making the right decision before deciding on a big life change.

Card	Keywords	Meaning	Reversed Meaning
1: The Magician	Manifestation, magick, creation, action, power, balance, skill and alchemy.	Trusting in yourself and the tools at your disposal. The Magician uses all four suits in the tarot and his creativity to manifest his dreams and desires.	Not having everything you need to manifest your goal.
2: The High Priestess	The Divine Feminine, intuition, power, awareness, creation, magick, wisdom, secret knowledge, psychic awareness and dreamwork.	Being intuitive and connected to the Universe and her magick. Connection to the Divine Feminine, and carrying this wisdom innately.	Disconnected from self and source (the Universe). The need to look inward to discover what you need to nurture and to reconnect with your spiritual self.
3: The Empress	The Divine Feminine or Goddess, nurturing, motherly, loving and creative.	Birthing something, and the expression of self and sensuality. The mother of the tarot.	Something needs more time to manifest. A need for nurturing energy.
4: The Emperor	Clarity, stability, action, power, success and self-discipline.	A need to use your power, logic and wit. Fairness and logic. The father figure of the tarot.	Overabuse of power, and unhealthy, authoritative power dynamics. Not enough structure.

Card	Keywords	Meaning	Reversed Meaning
5: The Hierophant	Spiritual wisdom, an advisor, teacher or guru and awareness.	A time of understanding and knowledge. You may encounter a teacher or someone who impacts your path.	You may be following others too closely or blindly. You must pay attention to what you believe and to what you know.
6: The Lovers	Love, relationships, happiness, sensuality, sexuality, abundance and emotional connections.	New or heightened romantic relationships or friendships. Your sensuality and sexuality are blooming, and love is coming.	A problem in a relationship, or the delay of love. Take time to learn about yourself and love yourself deeply before rushing into anything new.
7: The Chariot	Movement, guidance, direction, action, self-confidence and assurance.	Progress; being our own guiding force, trusting in our process and moving forward with our hearts and heads.	A need to find balance and stability before moving forward. Trust in yourself and your own abilities.
8: Strength	Strength, passion, fire, confidence and compassion.	Having the inner strength required to overcome any challenges. Connection to yourself and to courage, vitality and grace.	A need for more self-confidence and belief. Needing support from yourself and others.

Card	Keywords	Meaning	Reversed Meaning
9: The Hermit	Solitude, retreat, isolation, inner knowledge and wisdom.	Going from the material to the metaphysical. A change in values and goals resulting from time spent alone, observing yourself at a deep level.	You may be spending too much time alone. A need for community and connection.
10: Wheel of Fortune	Fate, fortune, karma, cycles, transition and change.	New opportunities are arising; change is coming. Karma is always being played out and the Wheel will keep turning.	There may be some turbulence and negativity in the future, but it's not permanent. If you're resisting change, see how it feels to let go.
11: Justice	Justice, balance, rewards, karma, fairness, truth and law.	Karma always keeping watch, getting our just desserts in the end.	A need to take responsibility for what you've done, recognizing your mistakes.
12: The Hanged Man	Shift in perspective, change, letting go and sacrifice.	A need to shift your perspective; a need to sacrifice or let go of something to get to higher ground.	It may be your perspective is holding you back. If you're overly attached to a situation or an outcome, try letting go.

Card	Keywords	Meaning	Reversed Meaning
13: Death	Endings, transformation, new beginnings, change and evolution.	Transformation in the most potent sense; one door is closing and another opening. Not actual death, but the cycle of life, death and rebirth.	You may be resisting the end of a natural cycle, even if you know it's time for it to end.
14: Temperance	Balance, patience, healing; go with the flow.	Balance is key. Taking time to restore to a state of equilibrium for your own well-being, especially before making a decision.	It may be time to recalibrate if things have become too much. You may need to restore the balance in a situation.
15: The Devil	Obsession, darkness, vices, being stuck, negativity and limitations.	It's important to indulge every now and then, but do not get carried away. Not handling moderation well.	Regaining control and learning the importance of balance and putting yourself first at times.
16: The Tower	Chaos, disruption, unexpected change, overthrow and new beginnings.	Create strong foundations before rebuilding. Everything falling apart so it can come back together.	Things aren't as bad as they seem. The hardest part is over and you're on the way out of this situation.

Card	Keywords	Meaning	Reversed Meaning
17: The Star	Hope, optimism, well-being, serenity, dreams manifesting, divine guidance and success.	Your dreams are answered and wishes come true. You are on a rewarding path: keep following your heart, intuition and dreams.	Don't get stuck in a cycle of negativity. Know that you can accomplish whatever you want. Keep moving toward your dreams.
18: The Moon	The subconscious, intuition, dreams, shadows and deception.	A connection to intuition and the Divine Feminine. An emphasis on psychic messages and shadow work.	You may be able to see truths and aspects of a situation that you couldn't before.
19: The Sun	Success, joy, happiness, radiance, energy and enthusiasm.	A joyous omen of completion and harvesting the fruits of your labor. Success, radiance and enthusiasm.	You may be having a hard time owning your success. You need to see past the clouds to enjoy the sun.
20: Judgment	Judgment, transformation, ending, reawakening and shifts.	Getting your just desserts. A critical time for self-reflection about the repeating patterns in your life that you need to resolve.	Your judgment may be off, which has caused you to miss out on an opportunity. Listen and learn from your intuition.
21: The World	Completion, success, ending a cycle and rebirth.	The completion of a major life cycle. Karma is on your side as you enter the next phase.	Now is the time to get things completed so you can move forward into a new state of abundance and rebirth.

the minor arcana

If the Major Arcana cards represent major transformation and the development of the human spirit, the Minor Arcana are the situations we face day-to-day. They're more mundane, relating to daily life, the people in it and situations that arise regularly.

The Minor Arcana cards have four suits, much like a deck of cards. These are the Wands (also known as Staffs), Cups (also known as Chalices), Swords (also known as Daggers) and Pentacles (also known as Discs or Coins). Each suit has ten cards and four court cards, starting at ace and rising to ten. Each suit, from ace to ten, represents a journey. They tell the story of a new beginning, movement forward, losing hope and then eventually coming out the other side. When you're first learning the tarot, or when you're buying a new deck, it's worth laying the cards out by suit in numerical order so you can see their progression and understand them as a story on a deeper level.

The court cards in the classic Rider-Waite are the Page, Knight, Queen and King. Some other decks will have a Prince and Princess instead of Page and Knight, while others have the Daughter, Son, Mother and Father. The Page has a sort of energy that is similar to the Fool's: slightly naïve, excited and ready for something new. The Knight is all about movement: he's on his horse, already on the way for what comes next. The Queen and the King represent their respective archetypes, energetically and/ or physically. The Queen is the more compassionate and intuitive of the two, while the King rules with his logic.

The court cards embody the energy of the suit they represent. In this way, we can form a deeper understanding of the tarot through the court cards, by relating to the real-life archetypes they embody. In addition to this, they can represent specific people or energies that we need to manifest. When these cards are reversed, they may act as a warning about an energy we shouldn't embody or an individual we should be aware of. If upside down, they also may signal that there's something holding us back from embodying the traits associated with them. If, when you read them, any of the cards in a spread are reversed, this may signify that their energy is inverted in some way.

wands

Wands are ruled by the Element of Fire. They relate to our inspiration, creativity and connection to the Universe. Wands are the messengers from our Higher Self that whisper in our ear in the form of new ideas. Wands are the instruments with which we manifest our desires, and thus represent our creative ventures, inspiration, passions and dreams. They're the suit of the spirit and the mind. When we pull a Wand card, it's often indicative of something that we haven't yet manifested in the physical realm, although the seed may already have been planted.

Card	Key Words	Meaning	Reversed Meaning
Ace	Inspiration, new beginnings, expansion, connection and creation.	A spark, a new beginning and the seed of a new project or idea.	A creative block and the need to step back and regroup before starting something new.
Two	Contemplation, determination, willpower, wisdom and following your own path.	A creative partnership or putting the action from the ace into the world.	Finding balance and taking time before moving on to the next thing.
Three	Self-reliance, inspiration, vision and expanding your horizons.	An homage to your own power and success. Looking and planning before acting.	Relying too much on others for direction, and a need to trust in yourself.
Four	Manifestation, celebration, joy, harmony, awareness and inner vision.	Take time to celebrate your achievements with loved ones, and recognize their part in your success.	An alternative approach to the situation is needed; utilizing your personal talents.
Five	Competition, delays, fighting, confusion and lack of direction.	Unnecessary drama and fighting for no reason.	Feeling caught up in drama that's not of your making, or being too passive about your needs.
Six	Good news, good fortune, victory and growth.	Things are getting better and you will rise up from the ashes; the drama lies behind you.	A setback in plans; almost through the thick of it but not yet.

Card	Key Words	Meaning	Reversed Meaning
Seven	Self-reliance, success within reach, courage and inner strength.	Don't give in to fighting; you already have an advantage over the other party; trusting in your truth is vital.	Holding on to situations that create tension and that no longer serve you.
Eight	Adventure, change, success, movement and news.	Focus on the task at hand, and honor the time and dedication needed for its completion.	If you don't get it together, you may lose out on an opportunity.
Nine	Stability, stamina, nearing the end of a journey, courage, trust and perseverance.	You are almost at the end of your journey: give yourself credit, and don't sell yourself short.	Overwhelmed and burned out, with something holding you back from completing the task at hand.
Ten	Overwhelmed, confused, trapped, darkness, overstimulation, blockage and difficulty.	Taking on too much at once; let something go before it becomes too overwhelming.	Avoiding responsibility, or taking on a responsibility that's not yours.
Page of Wands	Intuitive, courageous, optimistic, adventurous and visionary.	Someone adventurous and outgoing. New beginnings and opportunities and spiritual breakthroughs.	Someone who waits too long for things to happen: it's up to us to seize the day.

Card	Key Words	Meaning	Reversed Meaning
Knight of Wands	Fearless, confident, charming and adventurous.	A person filled with drive. Knowing how to balance emotions while being in tune with intuition.	Slow down and focus on the present before making any drastic decisions. Someone who's in over their head.
Queen of Wands	Spiritual, intuitive, vibrant, charismatic, generous and strong-willed.	Someone who's courageous, devoted and giving, with a radiant heart and a keen intellect. A reminder to follow your inspiration and passions.	Someone who asks for too much. Feelings of anger and violence or resentment.
King of Wands	Leader, visionary, charismatic, creative, capable and influential.	Someone who leads with their head and their heart. Tap into creativity as a form of art and healing.	This is someone who doesn't think of others or realize they're crossing the line. Impulsive behavior.

cups

Cups are ruled by the Element of Water and
represent anything and everything emotional:
our feelings, our subconscious and our intuition.
All matters of the heart are represented by this suit, which is the
most evocative and sensitive of the four; the energetic womb of
the tarot, so to speak. Cups symbolize our close relationships with
others, such as love and friendship.

Card	Keywords	Meaning	Reversed Meaning
Ace	New beginnings, new love, friendship and heightened psychic senses.	A new beginning of a deep nature, such as a romantic relationship or an intimate and loyal friendship.	Feeling emotionally depleted, sad and disconnected. A need for self-care.
Two	Romance, love, friendship, celebration, joy and bliss.	Romantic love, self-love and an exploration of all forms of love.	Possible heartbreak; the need for healing and self-love of all kinds.
Three	Friendship, community, celebration, joy, dancing and abundance.	Celebration with friends, basking in the joys of life and giving thanks as you celebrate.	Feeling disconnected from loved ones or community. A need to find healing with family and community.
Four	Apathy, boredom, scarcity and selfishness.	Coming from a place of scarcity and ingratitude.	Finally recognizing the gifts you've been given.

Card	Keywords	Meaning	Reversed Meaning
Five	Sadness, gloom, loss, pain, fear and self-pity.	Not being able to see through the grief or heartache, hurt and angst.	Finally seeing clearly, and moving through the pain and heartache.
Six	Children, family, childhood memories, connection and karmic connections.	Connection to childhood memories and memories of "home."	Issues from the past resurfacing; an invitation to heal past traumas.
Seven	Illusion, daydreaming, wishful thinking, deception and temptation.	Avoiding your real feelings through escapism and fantasy.	Dealing with your issues; starting to see your way out of the fog.
Eight	Abandonment, moving on, sacrifice and growth.	Moving forward out of necessity, through hurt, heartbreak and trauma, because there's no other choice.	Running away and avoidance as a form of escapism.
Nine	Fulfillment, wishes, kindness, abundance, satisfaction.	This is one of the most uplifting cards of the deck, and represents wishes coming true and abundance.	Feeling unfulfilled or like there's something missing.
Ten	Prosperity, abundance, fulfillment, spiritual growth, harmony and friendship.	A time of love and abundance, and being in tune with your spiritual and emotional needs.	Feeling uneasy or dissatisfied; not being fulfilled emotionally.

Card	Keywords	Meaning	Reversed Meaning
Page of Cups	Romantic, intuitive, understanding, free, emotional and young.	Someone intuitive and romantic who brings an open heart into whatever adventure they go on. Living from a place of love.	Emotions may be overwhelming to this person. Heartache, and the hurts of new love.
Knight of Cups	Open mind and heart, romantic and artistic; good news.	An artistic individual who follows their heart. Listening and manifesting with your intuition.	A closed-off heart and intuition; someone who does not trust easily.
Queen of Cups	Psychic, healing, introspective, loving, caring and thoughtful.	The most intuitive of the Queens, she feels before she "knows." Honoring your emotions.	Someone who's overly emotional and empathic, picking up on other people's energies unknowingly. A need to rekindle your creative energy.
King of Cups	Loyal, loving, devoted, protective and fierce.	The most intuitive of the Kings, a fair ruler who is connected to his head and his heart. A time of intense psychic connection and manifestation.	This person needs to calm their mind or their shadows will take over. A need to heal past traumas and trust your emotions and intuition.

swords

The suit of Swords is ruled by the Element of Air. Swords represent our thoughts, our decision-making, our intellect and the action we take when it comes to manifesting these decisions. The Swords also represent power dynamics, courage and conflict. They remind us that action can be constructive or destructive, and they tell us of the intersection between power and intellect. Swords are the most powerful and dangerous suit in the deck and remind us of the power of thought.

Card	Keywords	Meaning	Reversed Meaning
Ace	Mental clarity, truth, decision making, clarity and raw power.	Knowledge, like an "aha!" moment; newfound illumination and insight in the form of a new idea.	Lack of clarity and direction.
Two	Indecision, lack of direction, stalemate and unclear vision.	*The* card of indecision. To move forward you need to make a decision that you may be avoiding.	Confusion from an overwhelming sense of choice; being stuck between two competing sides.
Three	Heartbreak, sadness, hurt, harmful emotional ties and betrayal.	The card of heartbreak, warning of romantic entanglements that will end in pain.	The end of heartache; healing from past traumas and hurt to move forward.

Card	Keywords	Meaning	Reversed Meaning
Four	Stillness, mental clarity and power, rest and relaxation.	Focus on achieving clarity of thought before returning to the challenges before you.	Stagnation that leads to frustration, and the need to confront issues that are being avoided.
Five	Conflict, betrayal, self-destruction, loss.	A lack of direction; putting yourself down and in a place of harm that could be avoided.	Willingness to end a conflict. The fight is over and a new perspective is needed.
Six	Hope and a light at the end of the tunnel, progress; rite of passage.	Progress, after a long and hard road, toward a positive outcome; leaving tough situations behind.	Resisting this rite of passage and transition instead of letting go.
Seven	Deceit, sneaky betrayal and getting away with something.	Avoiding dealing with a situation by sneaking away from it.	Having no choice but to let go of things and situations that aren't serving you.
Eight	Trapped, blind, powerless, tied up and self-imposed boundaries.	Your own thoughts are trapping you, with self-imposed boundaries and a victim mind-set.	No longer playing the role of the victim; taking steps to reclaim your future.
Nine	Darkness, anguish, sadness, depression and nightmares.	The mental anguish and anxiety that come from purging unpleasant feelings to find healing at last.	At the end of pain and heartbreak, and finally seeing the light on the other side.

Card	Keywords	Meaning	Reversed Meaning
Ten	Pain, agony and anguish; backstabbing and defeat.	A difficult and painful ending; hitting rock bottom, but finally being able to start over or move on.	Dealing with past pain; healing and moving forward.
Page of Swords	Thoughtful, pensive, insightful and honest.	A keen observer. Notices everything; both insightful and logical.	Observing what is happening; using logic to make a plan.
Knight of Swords	Determined, ambitious, capable, energetic and action-oriented.	The initial momentum for a new idea or venture. A person who's naïve and impulsive.	A need to plan ahead—although this person might just need to learn this lesson on their own.
Queen of Swords	Insightful, loyal, determined, sharp-witted and intellectual.	This person is loyal, sharp, highly perceptive and very intellectual. Embrace being assertive and compassionate.	Listen to your brain as much as your heart, finding compassion in situations that others handle differently than you.
King of Swords	Authoritative, assertive, analytical, fair, disciplined and logical.	This person doesn't give in to emotional distraction, and is very communicative and able to understand people on a highly intellectual level.	This person may be deceptive and using power in a deceptive way. A need to be direct about their intentions.

pentacles

Pentacles are ruled by the Element of Earth. Pentacles represent everything physical in this realm: our homes, money, career and possessions. When a Pentacle comes up in a reading it's an indication of how we relate to the material world. Whether we're being too generous or greedy, too possessive or not careful enough, this suit reminds us of our basic, physical needs.

Card	Keywords	Meaning	Reversed Meaning
Ace	Prosperous new beginnings, triumph and financial gain.	New beginnings in the physical realm; could be a job, creative project or inspiration for something new.	Being overwhelmed/ burned out from taking on too much; now is not the time to start something new.
Two	Inevitable change, connection, receiving news, finding stability and balance.	A reminder of the inevitability of change; the importance of boundaries and to realign and reestablish them before moving forward.	Balance is needed, and an energetic exchange needs to take place for this to occur.
Three	Teamwork, dedication, craftsmanship, focus, specific skill set and community.	Working on something monumental, but relying on community to get it done.	Too much self-reliance, not having the specific skills or work ethic to complete a certain task alone.

Card	Keywords	Meaning	Reversed Meaning
Four	Possession, ownership, control and unexpected opposition.	Being too rigid and attached to the physical realm as a source of happiness, as well as being stingy.	Redefining success and wealth; relinquishing control of possessions; a delay in material gain.
Five	Worry, loss, scarcity, lack of direction and/or security and poverty.	Heading down a path that doesn't support your needs; accept loss in order to finally move on.	The end of a time of loss and poverty; coming out of a dark time.
Six	Prosperity, growth, having plenty, hard work paying off and sharing.	The fruits of your labor manifesting and finally being ready to harvest.	Jealousy; having the mentality of scarcity, and not sharing the gifts you've been given.
Seven	Contemplation, standing still, evaluation and taking the long-term view.	A period of contemplation and hard work in order to find stability.	Investing time and energy into something that will not sustain you in the end; not taking responsibility for your own needs.
Eight	Skill, labor, craftsmanship, dedication to the craft, apprenticeship.	Dedication and commitment to excellence in a craft.	The need to hone your specific skill and learn.
Nine	Long-term stability; health and happiness; a comfortable and stable home.	A card of long-term luxury that proves that our hard work and dedication to our craft has paid off.	A loss or setback that could have been avoided.

Card	Keywords	Meaning	Reversed Meaning
Ten	Abundance, fulfillment, wealth, retirement, permanence and lasting success.	A promise of success, achievement, pride and stability as a result of hard work.	Financial loss and lack of resources and stability, and being unsure of the future.
Page of Pentacles	Kind, responsible, supportive, dreamer and visionary.	Someone who is both grounded and introverted. Slowing down before making a decision.	Prioritize actions in pursuit of your goals.
Knight of Pentacles	Hardworking, dedicated, calm, stubborn and loyal.	This person is extremely loyal and dedicated, very driven and ambitious. The ability to get things completed.	Feelings of stagnation linger; a need for adventure and risk.
Queen of Pentacles	Generous, caring, nurturing and loving; a healer.	Motherly and nurturing, with many qualities of a healer. She is a supportive and grounding presence who's both wise and loving.	A need to ground your energies, and to tap into some inner nurturing.
King of Pentacles	Steady, grounded, loyal and family-oriented.	Grounded and passionate, and often incredibly successful in their career. Ambitious and gives honest and clear advice.	This may represent a person who is possessive and authoritative. A need for stillness in Nature.

read the cards

The first thing to keep in mind with the tarot is that there's no "right" way to read. Yes, it's important to know the archetypes and symbols associated with the cards and what these represent, but there are layers to each card, and these will be expressed in different ways in different readings, depending on who you're reading for and their question. You will also learn more about the cards as you work with them. At first it may seem scary to read the cards, but believing in your intuition will give you stronger readings, I promise. Creating your own ritual for reading your cards is important too, and this will develop over time. Here are some simple steps to get you started:

STEP 1: CLEANSE THE CARDS

It's important to regularly cleanse your cards! Tarot cards pick up the energy of whoever is having their cards read, so cleansing is essential if you're reading for other people. I prefer to use sage and palo santo to smudge my cards, but you can leave a piece of selenite, a self-cleansing crystal, on top of your deck instead. You can also smudge with mugwort to help you open your psychic channel. To do this, imagine a door opening at the crown of your head, and ask for any messages from your cosmic team to come through in this way.

STEP 2: ASK A QUESTION

Before any tarot reading, the querent (the person whose cards are being read) will ask a question. If you're reading for yourself then *you'll* ask a question. Try something broad like "what does the future hold for my love life?" or "what do I need to know about this job offer?" You can also focus on a specific topic like love or money. Sometimes you have to ask a "yes" or "no" question, and that's okay, but the cards aren't always that cut and dry! After you choose a question you'll pick a layout that examines this question further.

STEP 3: PICK A SPREAD

Tarot spreads are a way to gain information from the deck, and a spread is created when you physically lay out the cards in a particular sequence. Besides addressing an overarching question, each card in the spread will address specific issues, depending on where it is positioned. (I also like to see which card is lying at the bottom of the deck: this card represents the underlying message of the reading and often adds some unexpected insight.) Take a look at the spreads on pages 130–32, and choose the method that seems the best fit for your question.

STEP 4: BREATHE AND SHUFFLE WITH INTENTION

Take a second to breathe and ground. Connect to the Earth and ask for guidance. Take a few deep breaths, then shuffle the deck, or if reading for another, ask the querent to do this. You can shuffle in any way you like: like a regular card deck, or with the cards on their side. As you shuffle, focus on your question. When you feel ready, cut the deck: split it into two piles and put the second pile on top.

STEP 5: LAY OUT THE CARDS

Start to pull the cards and place them in the positions based on your chosen spread. Refer to the interpretations of the cards on pages 106–25, as well as your gut feeling and any symbols that come up. You can also refer to the guidebook that comes with the deck. See how the question and the layout relate to the interpretation of the card. Honor what you feel. If necessary to help clarify something, pull an extra card. And don't be afraid to do more research on a card if you get stuck. When you've finished interpreting the cards individually, try to see how they fit together as a whole.

STEP 6: TAKE NOTES AND RECORD

Take notes of the cards and the layout. I like to keep a tarot journal specifically for my readings, recording any insight and interpretations that come up.

STEP 7: GROUND AND CENTER

After a reading, make sure you ground your energy, grounding through the base of your spine. If you imagined a door opening at the crown of your head, imagine it closing now while thanking your cosmic team for any insight or guidance they offered. Take your cards and put them in a safe place until next time.

tarot spreads

Reading the tarot can be as simple as pulling a card a day, or it can take the form of elaborate spreads. Here are some spreads to get you started.

TAROT A DAY KEEPS THE DOCTOR AWAY

A really easy and accessible way to learn to read the cards is to work with them by pulling a card each day. I suggest doing this first thing in the morning, so you can see how the card's energy manifests in the day's events. You can take a photo of your card and make it your phone background, or carry it around with you. I like to pull a card or two each morning and then go back through all of the cards I've pulled that week on a Sunday night, to see how my week has gone. By becoming familiar with the way in which certain events correlate to certain cards, you'll learn the tarot in a more concrete way.

THREE-CARD SPREADS

An easy way to work with the cards is to pull three cards. The most common three-card spread is past/present/future, where the first card pulled represents the past, the second the present and the third the future, all pertaining to the question being asked. This spread can also be adapted and used to represent mind/body/spirit or address a variety of other queries. Three cards can also be used to gain more clarity about the question being asked.

THE CELTIC CROSS

The most classic card layout, however, has to be the ten-card Celtic Cross. This spread examines where you are in relation to your question, any external or internal influences and the potential outcome of the situation. It's a very thorough and very accurate spread. Every tarot reader will have their own variation of this spread, so play around with what each card represents until you find something that clicks. In a traditional spread, the positions of the cards have the following significance:

1. You.

2. What's crossing or blocking you.

3. The unconscious cause.

4. Recent past.

5. The outcome if something changes.

6. The immediate future.

7. Your power.

8. External influences and energies.

9. Hopes and fears.

10. The final outcome.

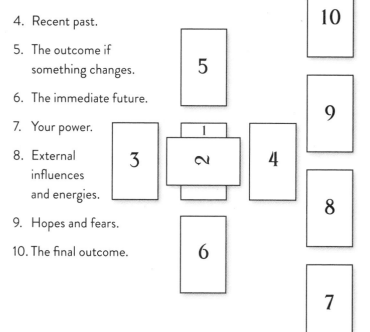

THE ELEMENT SPREAD

This spread uses the energies of the Elements to help give you perspective and guidance. You can call on the Elements before using this spread in a reading or you can simply use it on its own. The positions are:

1. You.

2. Earth: what grounds you.

3. Air: what guides you.

4. Fire: what fuels you.

5. Water: what supports/sustains you.

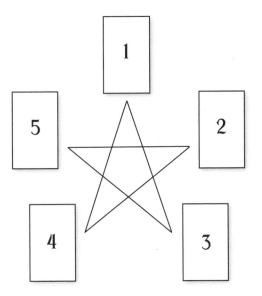

A TAROT SPELL TO HELP YOU HEAL KARMIC WOUNDS

This spell is best done on the new or waning Moon. It utilizes tarot cards and candle magick to help you focus your energy and heal karmic wounds. Karmic wounds are wounds caused in past lifetimes. By healing them we allow for more freedom in this lifetime.

If, for example, you've ever had an intense connection with someone, even though you're not sure why, or if you feel like you've known them for years when you haven't, you may have a karmic connection. If you didn't heal fully from your relationship with that person in the past, you might still carry these sorts of soul wounds in your heart. Similarly, if you're terrified of something for no reason, or feel very intense sadness or grief over something that's never happened to you, you may have karmic wounds. The spell that follows will help to dissolve this pain, cleansing your soul, so hopefully you'll feel lighter and less connected and obstructed by your relationship to the person or thing and the intense feelings that come along with it.

Tarot cards: pick two tarot cards that represent whatever it is you want to let go of and what you want to attract. The Devil, the Lovers, the Tower, the three of Swords and Death might work well, but any cards you're drawn to will also work. Pick cards that resonate with what you're healing; if it concerns love, for instance, you may wish to pick the three of Swords and the Lovers, whereas if it's about a bad habit you need to banish, you may wish to pick the Devil and the Ten of Pentacles.

You will also need: sage, palo santo or another herb for smudging; a lighter; a black candle and a white votive candle and something safe to burn them in; a pencil or pin to write on your candle; rue and rosemary for protection and lavender for healing; a shower; your grimoire to record anything that comes up. *Optional:* amethyst for healing, tourmaline for protection, rose quartz for love.

» Cleanse your space using your chosen herbs.

» Set up an altar with the black and white candles and your chosen tarot cards in front of them. You can have your herbs, grimoire, any crystals you're using and lighter.

» Take a ritual shower. Undress slowly and intentionally, paying attention to your breathing. As you step into the shower, continue breathing rhythmically. Imagine that the warm water cascading over you is healing you with every drop. You can also imagine you're under a fountain of healing light that's cleansing you. Enjoy the moment, and when you're done, step out of the shower.

» Put on something comfortable that makes you feel powerful and move to your altar.

» Cast a circle of protection around your space, asking your guides, masters or deities for their healing and compassion.

» Meditate with the tarot cards. Look at your chosen cards, allowing your gaze to soften. Continue to breathe rhythmically, finding a sense of peace in your breath. Take this time to focus on what these cards mean to you and how they represent what you want to heal.

» Using your pin or pencil, write what you want to release on the black candle. It can be a word or a phrase, like "emotional attachment" or "addiction" or "hate." As you carve, imagine all the energy infusing into the candle.

» Do the same thing on the white candle, writing what you hope to gain and manifest. It can be a word like "healing" or "love." As you inscribe your candle, imagine an overwhelming feeling of bliss and of release that comes with whatever you're healing.

» Surround the candles with the rue and rosemary while asking for protection, and with lavender, asking for healing.

» Light the candles, calling in healing and compassion. Imagine all the hurt melting away with the black candle. Imagine the white candle inviting in lifetimes of healing. Let your gaze soften as you sit with these. You can gaze at your tarot cards as well, holding the imagery in your mind's eye.

» Record anything that comes up in your grimoire.

» If it's safe to do so, let the candles burn all the way down. If not, use a candle snuffer or a fan to put them out.

» Close the circle and ground your energy, pressing your forehead into the Earth.

» Dispose of the wax at a crossroads or intersection.

In the days that follow, pay attention to your dreams and any psychic information that comes up in them. If this happens, make a note of it in your grimoire or tarot journal. Listen to your intuition and see what it says. Let this lead you! You can also look up the symbolism of what you saw in a dream dictionary.

CHAPTER FOUR

the veil of glamour: fashion magick

When you want to feel powerful, magickal or like a witch who knows what she wants . . . what do you put on? Maybe you wear a vintage blouse that your mother gave to you. Maybe you slip on your coziest oversized black tee. Perhaps you'll put on some leather, or something that makes you feel unstoppable.

To deny the power in clothing is to deny its own special magick. It's not because of what it looks like or because it's designer. It's simply because we wear clothing every day, and many of our ancestors did too. And if they didn't usually wear much clothing, whatever clothing they did wear was sacred.

Much like magick, fashion has to evolve to stay relevant. Even if we're not into fashion, even if we don't care much about style or the happenings in the fashion industry, we're still surrounded by it and exposed to it by our peers, social media, the internet and so on. Magick is similar. When it doesn't evolve with the time and its people, it ceases to be relevant, necessary and as impactful as it can be. And if our magick is about more than the spells and rituals we cast, if it's actually the way in which we live our life and how we relate to those around us, and if we live our life in clothing, wouldn't it make sense to combine the two?

fashion magick

Fashion magick works at the intersection of style, beauty and glamour. Fashion magick means being intentional with your clothing, and using magick to infuse what you wear with some energy. It doesn't mean you have to get dressed up every day. It just means you see your clothing as an opportunity to imbue magick further into your life, and to connect with your own ancestors in yet another way.

glamour as more than glamour

While we may be used to hearing the word "glamorous" to describe someone who's dressed to the nines, looking all sorts of posh, the truth is this word itself is historically rooted in magick and enchantment. A "glamour" is a veil that disguises what lies beneath, concealing the real version of something. Faeries are said to use glamour when they appear to us as something other than their true selves.

And the truth is, glamour as we know it isn't far from the glamour of magick. When I fill in my eyebrows and draw on a cat eye so sharp it can kill a man, I'm casting a glamour. When I swipe on some rouge and some bright red lipstick, I'm casting a glamour. By curating how others see me, by *deciding* how I want others to see me, I'm casting a glamour. When I wear my favorite black netted dress with my Vivienne Westwood "Sex" bag and my favorite high heels, I am casting a glamour; one that says: "I am powerful, I'm in charge and you do not want to mess with me." You cast a glamour in the same way every time you put on something that makes you feel more powerful and more embodied than without it. Maybe sexy is powerful to you, maybe high femme is, maybe no makeup and all denim is; it doesn't matter what you wear as much as the feeling you get when you're dressed in a true-to-you look.

fashion as spiritual armor

As women and femmes, we face a battle every day when we step outside our homes. For some reason, men think that they're entitled to tell us what they think of us, catcalling us with "compliments" that we're supposed to appreciate. Goddess forbid we wear something vaguely revealing or unusual. Then they really feel entitled to give us their opinions.

Fashion as spiritual armor means wearing an outfit because you want to, regardless of what anyone else thinks. It's wearing that spiked choker and grabbing your tourmaline when you don't want anybody to mess with you. It's wearing a sheer blue slip and silver eyeliner when you want to channel the Moon and the ocean. It's

SEE YOUR
STYLE AS A FORM
OF SPIRITUAL
ARMOR THAT
YOU CAN TAKE
WITH YOU
ANYWHERE,
ANYTIME.

drawing protective symbols on the labels of your clothing to keep you safe as you travel to faraway places.

Magick is all about how you feel, and so is fashion. Everyone knows how it feels to slip into something that makes them feel amazing. It's powerful. By combining this with a healthy dose of magick, we're able to infuse our everyday life with more power. See your style as a form of spiritual armor that you can take with you anywhere, anytime.

your fashion chakra

I like to think of working with fashion magick as being like working with your fashion chakra, although in some respects the fashion chakra is more like your aura, lying closest to your skin, though the fashion chakra isn't a recognized energy center like the other chakras. When you start to work with fashion as a conscious manifestation of your inner magick, you'll notice subtle pushes about what to wear or whether to embody something. Suddenly, you'll want to wear everything in the color orange—but only with red lipstick on. Maybe you'll feel the urge to embody the assertiveness of the leather jacket. As you allow yourself to explore your style in a way that permits it to evolve and change cyclically like you do, you'll notice that you'll become surer of yourself, more confident, more assertive in who you are.

Your fashion chakra isn't fed by money or designer labels. She's fed when she's dressed and loved intentionally; when the perfect piece finds her at the thrift store, or when a gift finds its way to her. Work with your fashion chakra by experimenting with your style. Try wearing a new color or new silhouette. Look into vintage styles, clear out your closet and go thrifting. Experiment and keep your findings in a journal for future reference.

a magick morning routine

Each day, we have the opportunity to set ourselves up to live from a place of effortless unfolding. Although it can be really hard sometimes to wake up and find the motivation or the time to get ready before going to school or work, if you turn your morning routine into a ritual, it becomes easier. Think of each morning as being like an offering to yourself and to the Universe. If you set your day up to be infused with magick, then the Universe has no choice but to answer that call.

cosmic inspiration for your day

Two of my favorite ways to infuse my day with magick are to see which astrological sign the Moon is in and to draw my daily tarot card as inspiration for my outfit and makeup. I also like to match my makeup or outfit to crystals and flowers for some extra Earth energy. To help you decide where to draw your inspiration from, you might also find it useful to be aware of which sign the Sun is in, as well as what you're feeling each morning.

THE MOON

The Moon rules over our emotional body, our unconscious mind and the Divine Feminine in each of us. She pulls at the ocean of our souls and whispers secrets into our hearts. By finding out which astrological sign the Moon is in (see Chapter 7), you will have a cosmic blueprint of the energies of the day ahead, and can draw additional inspiration for whatever look you want to create based on what you feel. I use the app TimePassages to keep track of the Moon's sign, but there are plenty of other apps and online sources to help you keep track of her too.

For example, as I'm writing this, the Moon is in the sign of Cancer. Cancer is ruled by the Moon, and its symbol is the crab. Cancers are emotional, sensitive and feel things very deeply. I'm also PMSing, so I've been feeling extra emotional as well. To combat this, I've decided to wear silver eyeshadow to channel the Moon, and my favorite long-sleeve black dress with my pentacle necklace as a way to protect myself from any extra emotions that aren't mine. I also wear a lot of pink when the Moon is in a water sign (read: tenderhearted and emo *af*).

TAROT

One of my favorite ways to connect to the tarot is to use it for fashion and beauty inspiration. In the morning after waking up, I'll take some time to breathe and connect with my guides as I shuffle and pull my daily tarot card or cards. I'll use this as inspiration for my makeup or my outfit.

There's no wrong way to connect with the cards, so be creative with your interpretation of whichever card you pull, focusing on the energy, or a detail in its artwork. By embodying the energies of your daily tarot cards through what you wear you're sure to form a strong relationship with them.

CRYSTALS

You can also find makeup and outfit inspiration through working with crystals (see Chapter 7). Whether you wear a sheer pink dress with a stellar highlight and blush lipstick to channel the love of rose quartz or an entirely black ensemble for protective tourmaline, Mother Earth can become your muse. You can also wear the stone whose properties you're embodying or carry some around with you to really work with this energy.

color code it

Besides finding fashion inspiration in the tarot, Moon and the natural world, you can also find it in the colors of the clothing and makeup you choose to wear.

Wear this (or shades of this) . . .	To feel this . . .
Red	Passionate, fierce, capable, connected to the Element of Fire and the first chakra, dangerous, sexy and sensual.
Pink	Loved, loving, compassionate, connected to your heart, happy, vivacious and confident.
Orange	Passionate, creative, connected to your second chakra and the Element of Fire.
Yellow	Rich, wealthy, loving, creative, visionary, bright, happy, connected to the third chakra and the Sun.

Wear this (or shades of this) . . .	To feel this . . .
Green	Creative, connected to the heart chakra and the Earth, inspired, calm, content, loving and compassionate.
Blue	Calm, connected to the throat chakra and the Element of Water, able, serene, goddess-like, vibrant and effortless.
Purple	Royal, divine, psychic, connected to the third eye, knowledgeable, noteworthy, memorable, like a queen—mystical and ravishing.
Black	Transformative, powerful, secure, sexy, mysterious, mystical, badass and sensual.
White	Serene, pure, loving, connected to your Higher Self, positive and calm.
Neutrals	Adaptable, secure, comfortable, connected to the Earth, calm, capable and centered.
Metallics/ holographic	Otherworldly, divine, like an alien, connected to crystals, connected to the Universe and the Moon.

makeup as ritual

If fashion is resistance, then beauty is ritual. For me, my skin care and makeup routine are the first things I do in the morning after waking up. I wash my face, brush my teeth and start on my routine. Usually, I know where the Moon and Sun are, and I've already started to feel the energy of the day. Doing my makeup is the first piece of putting on my glamour. Do I feel like channeling an open heart, or working with a fierce attitude? Do I want to wear gold to attract abundance, or do I want to wear red to feel dangerous? Sometimes you don't have enough time to be this intentional and that's totally okay! There are no rules—and we are cyclical too, remember?

If you wear makeup, try honoring the process of putting it on as a ritual. Turn on some music, burn some incense, spray on some perfume and get to work. You can also create a beauty altar in your bathroom, or on a vanity table, as further ways to channel energy. Try adding crystals, photos of style icons, old starlets or family members to this; there's no wrong way to do it.

The first thing to ask when beginning your makeup ritual is "what do I feel like today?" For example:

» A cat eye, drawn with eyeliner, is a perfect glamour for when you don't want people to mess with you.

» A silver eye is the ultimate way to honor the Moon.

» Dark green and gold eye makeup can help you channel Mother Nature in an organic way.

» A kiss of blush can help attract love and sex, since blush mimics the flush of an orgasm!

You can also work with the colors from the earlier chart and then get creative. If you like, think about what sort of makeup the women in your family—either chosen or blood—wear. Want to channel your mother's confidence? Why not wear her red lip? How about your aunt's spontaneity? Try wearing her green eyeliner, or whatever her signature look is.

And if you want to infuse some extra blessings into your routine, try using mantras while you're working on your makeup. You can create your own mantras (which I encourage since this is *your* path) or use one of the following, listed on the next page. You can also sit for a second once your makeup is completed, visualizing whatever it is you hope your day holds. Hold this in your third eye for a second and then imagine it turning into a bubble that floats into the Universe. So it is!

As you do this . . .	Say this . . .
Face	May I face the day with _____ (love, an open heart, courage, presence, stillness, passion, energy, joy, bliss, respect, etc.).
Eyebrows	May I frame my day with _____ (truth, love, honesty, compassion, etc.).
Eyes	May I follow my truth and know what's real. May I see _____ (the best of the situation, love, joy, etc.).
Eyeliner	No one can mess with me; I am centered and I am ready.
Lips	From these lips shall spill the truth, compassion, love and spells of healing.
Cheeks	And by these cheeks I shall smile truthfully, knowing that the Universe cares and protects me.

spiritual style

One of the amazing things about fashion is that there's always something waiting to inspire you. Whether it's the silhouette of a palm tree against an ice-blue sky, a barrier-breaking runway show, an ethereal piece of art or an animal, all you have to do is open your third eye and wait for the Universe to guide you. You can turn this inspiration into a spiritual practice by creating a spiritual style of your own—one that helps you embody who you want to be physically, emotionally, spiritually and mentally. And by picking a style archetype, aka a fashion spirit guide, you'll have some cosmic guidance for your style choices.

the archetypes of fashion

Would you like to find a style muse? Someone you can call upon and channel whenever you walk into a room and need to feel confident? By working with a fashion archetype, you can draw inspiration not only from that person themselves, but also from the archetype and energy the person embodies. Whether you're looking to tap into your inner queen or your sacred sexuality, think of your style archetype as a style spirit guide to call upon and channel for some extra glamour.

Take the time to search the web, magazines and bookstores for someone who catches your eye. Take special note if this person appears more than once; they could be calling to you. Go on Pinterest, visit a museum, look at old books—get creative.

THE QUEEN: VIVIENNE WESTWOOD

Dame Vivienne Westwood embodies the power, elegance and strength of the Queen archetype. Vivienne Westwood is a British fashion designer who helped pioneer the punk movement. After splitting from her creative and romantic partner Malcolm McLaren in the 1970s, Vivienne went on to establish her own fashion house. Known for its expert use of corsets and silhouettes, its unapologetic style and its extensive references to art and art history, Vivienne's work is both eccentric and purposeful, with an underlying theme of rebellion that she's carried with her since her punk days. Today, Vivienne, who was made a dame by Queen Elizabeth II, makes sure each of her runway shows has a political message, whether it's to stop fracking or to switch to sustainable energy. Vivienne uses fashion as a way to start conversations and incite true reform. Even now, in her late seventies, with her head of fiery red hair and her fierce spirit, Vivienne isn't slowing down anytime soon. If you need a reminder that age doesn't mean shit, that it's fun to wear crazy outfits and that you can use what you love to make a difference, then call on Queen Viv.

To channel Vivienne's energy and style: embrace tartan; safety pins; tutus; Doc Martens; hair dye; your own personal style and fashion as activism.

THE MOTHER: BEYONCÉ

Is there anything Beyoncé can't do? Yes, she's also a Queen in her own right (which is where I was going to put her originally), but she's also the Empress and the Mother. She is passionate, she's vocal, she's sexual and she's unapologetic. Many of us are taught that once we have kids (*if* we have kids), we're supposed to turn off our sexuality and turn on our maternal instincts. Queen B proves this isn't necessary: you can have both and then some. With her jaw-dropping looks, her sultry dance numbers and her refusal to stay silent in the face of injustice, Beyoncé is the ultimate Mother. Not only is she protective of her kin, she's protective of herself and her own needs, not to mention her fans and their needs too. She's also a vocal activist, has incredible style and is an amazing mother; so why wouldn't you want to channel her?

To channel Beyoncé's energy and style: wear contrasting patterns and strong colors; embrace your femininity at any age and show it off with sensual and strong silhouettes.

THE SEXPOT: DITA VON TEESE

If there's anyone who knows how to use glamour and unabashed sexuality to make a statement, it's Dita Von Teese. The stripper turned burlesque performer is as known for her Swarovski-encrusted outfits as she is for her tiny waist. Dita has made a name for herself with her elaborate burlesque routines and shows that are theatrical, sexy and oh so Hollywood. Dita literally gets paid to take her clothes off and she embraces it. In her mid-forties, she's still at the top of her game, using dance, theater, fashion and her signature makeup to cast a glamour. Dita's sexual and sultry—and she's unapologetic about it. If you want to channel your inner Sexpot, put on some beautiful lingerie and your favorite record, and do a striptease for no one except yourself—or whoever else you deem lucky enough to watch.

To channel Dita's energy and style: wear lace; satin; corsets; vintage lingerie; silks; pinup-style clothing and your own signature hair and makeup look.

THE ARTIST: PATTI SMITH

Patti Smith is the embodiment of what it means to be an Artist through and through. After moving to New York as a teenager in the 1970s, Patti worked odd jobs, eventually making a name for herself after her debut album, *Horses,* was released. Not only is Patti a poet and musician, she's also a writer and an artist who lived in the iconic Chelsea Hotel. Patti's known for her laid-back style. She's the ultimate muse and Artist archetype because she doesn't only create art, she embodies it. No matter what she's wearing, Patti embodies a sense of freedom that many of us are still looking for today.

To channel Patti's energy and style: use a special item of clothing such as a certain T-shirt every time you paint; write love letters on your clothing; listen to her music; think messy hair, white T-shirts and her wardrobe staple—the leather jacket.

THE WITCH: STEVIE NICKS AND ERYKAH BADU

Both of these women embody the energy of the witch; they're fearless, magickal, glamorous and entrancing. Every woman in this section has their own magick about them, but Stevie and Erykah have a specific way of weaving their essence into their art that is unparalleled. While Stevie has talked about her love of witches, though never publicly identified herself as one, Erykah has openly embraced the title and her own form of the craft. Both women are more than musicians, using their brand of magick to create personas that embody the mystical. By working with fashion and costuming, they've created a divine essence that is more than just a performance. They truly live their magick, and it's seen in what they wear, what they sing and the art they create. These women remind us that sometimes all we need to stand in our power is a bewitching outfit and an air of mystery.

To channel Stevie's and Erykah's energy and style: wear floaty dresses; caftans; loud head scarves; use tambourines as accessories; dress in loose and flowing silhouettes.

THE LOVER: MORTICIA ADDAMS

Is there really anyone who embodies the essence of the lover more than Morticia Addams? Even though she may be a mother and a wife, Morticia still takes pleasure in pleasure. Not just open in her desires, she's vocal about them too. Does Morticia want Gomez to frighten her like a demon? Does she want to play in the dungeon? Absolutely, and she's not afraid to say it! Morticia is aware of her power; she simply has to speak French and Gomez loses his mind, kissing up and down her arm as he continues to fall even more hopelessly in love with her. The two together are like the Lovers tarot card, showing the yin and yang of a relationship and the love that must come from both sides. Morticia reminds us of the power of the black dress, as well the power of developing your own signature style. She also reminds us of the power of living with an open heart and open mind. Call on her when you want to embody the energy of the Lover or to develop a signature style of your own.

To channel Morticia's energy and style: wear a black dress; rose perfume; red lipstick; anything that makes you feel like your own lover.

THE GODDESS: VENUS

If you ever want to feel like the otherworldly creature you are, just think of Venus. Birthed from the sea foam, this goddess spends her days being tended to, fed, cared for and adored. Venus is beauty embodied; she reminds us of the pleasure and pure energy of sensuality. She asks us to step into our bodies and honor them simply because we exist. She also invites us to turn our lives into a ritual, honoring the divine inside of us that is reflected in the Universe. Venus is soft; she's loving, curvy, full and beautiful. She reminds us that there's no shame in loving our own bodies, and dressing ourselves in the offerings of the Earth. Venus is beauty personified, and she can serve as a wonderful muse for anyone looking to connect their sensuality and beauty to their everyday life. Stand at the edge of the ocean and call on Venus for her blessing. Open your heart a little more each day to channel this goddess archetype.

To channel Venus's energy and style: wear shells; the colors of the sea at sunset; tulle; ocean jasper; pink lipstick and blush.

accessorize your look

talismans

As I mentioned in the introduction, another way to literally wear your magick is by working with talismans. This is perfect if you already have jewelry that's of sentimental value to you and that you wear all the time. And even if you don't, you can still create a talisman. A talisman is a protective amulet that you keep with you throughout the day. It serves as a focal point for energy as well as a protective barrier against negativity.

Think about what you need more of in your everyday life. Whether you need to be more vocal and assertive, or more calm and Zen, you can find a talisman that fulfills your intention. If you're combining a necklace with a crystal or pentacle, or a pendant with some other spiritual motif on it, then that energy will also be incorporated into the talisman. You can bless this jewelry the same way you might bless your clothing (see page 159). To charge your talisman, see the instructions on page 219, and pick whatever intention you want, infusing that into your piece.

honoring your ancestors

We carry the story of our ancestors in our bones. We are here because of those who came before us. We are built on the shoulders of the women and men who allowed us to be where we are today. A really beautiful way to give thanks to our ancestors is by working with heirlooms and talismans. I love jewelry because it's easy to wear regularly, and because it's so often passed from generation to generation, but this sort of talisman can take the form of anything you can wear or carry with you: a vintage handbag, a coin purse from a foreign place, a pin or brooch, a beloved jacket.

Do you have a ring of your grandmother's that you can wear when you need to be reminded of her resilience? How about a necklace passed down for generations in your family? What about your mother's vintage purse or your great-grandpa's pocket watch? Even if your heirloom or talisman isn't given to you by a blood relative, these pieces can still offer support and guidance. They are a reminder that we still carry the spirit of our loved ones with us and that all we have to do is call on them, or wear these pieces, when we need them.

You can charge these pieces the same way as a talisman or an item of clothing, and add them to your altar. This would be an especially appropriate practice for the festival of Samhain, as a way to channel the energy and spirit of your loved ones. However, you can create an altar to honor your ancestors at any time you wish. Place the pieces that connect you to your ancestors on your altar and incorporate them in the setup by thinking about what this person liked. If they had a favorite flower, candy, liquor, herb, scent or color, you can decorate your altar accordingly.

my story

Part of my journey with witchcraft—specifically with fashion magick—is very personal. Fashion and fashion magick are in my blood. I wouldn't be here if it weren't for my family's relationship with clothing and textiles.

My paternal grandmother, Rose Weiss, survived three years in the concentration camps because of her work as a seamstress. As fate would have it, she had the same name as the head seamstress's niece at Auschwitz and, because she was actually trained in sewing, was able to stay in the seamstresses' quarters of the camp, sewing and repairing uniforms for the Nazis and their families. She was able to get work for her sister Edith as well. She wrote a memoir about her experiences, and from it I learned that her father and uncle owned a fur business.

After the war, Rose met my grandpa Harry when he was training her in how to load anti-missile cannons for the Haganah, the Jewish paramilitary organization that went on to become the Israel Defense Forces. Apparently, the first thing he ever said to her was, "If you don't mind me telling you, soldier, your fly's open." Before Harry was sent to the concentration camps, which

he also endured for three years, he had been apprenticed in Prague to become a master weaver.

On the other side of the family, my maternal great-grandparents escaped Poland before the war and fled to Mexico City, where they started a store that sold things like gloves and tights. Eventually they started a zipper factory, as well as a family.

My background is in fashion writing, and I am very passionate about using clothing as a way not only to express myself, but to connect with my soul purpose. As someone who's ethnically Jewish, and had more than seventy members of her family in concentration camps, I shouldn't be here. Yet I still am. I honor this by connecting to my ancestors through what I wear and by incorporating fashion into my magick. I am so thankful to be able to continue this through this book.

A BLESSING TO PROTECT YOU AND YOUR CLOTHING, AND YOUR ACCESSORIES

Most mornings, we put on our clothes and face the world head-on, heart open. Yet regardless of your spiritual practice, there are days when you might just need a little extra support and guidance. We can ask the Universe for help *whenever we need.* And we can bless our clothing for extra protection as well.

The best time to do this blessing is in the morning, before you put the items of clothing on. You can also charge your clothing by placing it on your altar the night before and placing crystals like labradorite (to cleanse and protect your aura), selenite (to absorb negativity), amethyst (for healing), rose quartz (for love) and clear quartz (to enhance the other stones) on it.

Step 1: Cleanse.

Smudge your clothing with palo santo, sweetgrass, mugwort or sage. You can also wave a selenite wand around it to absorb any negative energy. Take a second to breathe and ground into your feet, connecting with your root chakra.

Step 2: Bless it up.

Take a few deep breaths, asking for connection and guidance from your ancestors, spirit guides, masters, deities or whatever other beings you work with. Breathe into this place of connection and knowing. Place your hands on what you're charging and then say something along the following lines as you imagine white light seeping into the clothes:

> "I bless these clothes on this day; may they help me move safely. May the Universe provide for me clothing that protects and heals my energy. May my ancestors hear my call to bless these garments and the skin they lie upon. By the blessing in me, so it is and so it shall be."

Remember, these words are only a suggestion. Say whatever feels most powerful to you! Take a second to breathe into this space, ground your energy and then put your clothing on. Voilà!

If you like this blessing, you can buy a special candle to light whenever you do it. A pillar candle would be perfect.

FIRE WALK WITH ME: A SHOE SIGIL SPELL FOR PROTECTION

This spell works by placing a protective symbol called a sigil on the sole of your shoe. This charms the shoe for protection, allowing you to navigate both familiar and unfamiliar territory safely.

This spell is best done on a new, full or waxing Moon. This is an especially good spell to do before traveling to a new place or environment.

You will need: a pair (or multiple pairs) of shoes; a black Sharpie or a permanent marker; a pencil and paper; salt.

Step 1: Ground and center.

Take a second to ground. Breathe into the space at your root chakra, feeling this energy extend into the soul of the Earth. Imagine feeling safe and supported and protected, like harm cannot befall you no matter what. Then breathe this energy into your feet. Imagine white light flowing directly from the Earth into your soles, protecting you whenever you take a step.

Step 2: Cast the circle.

Cast your circle, as described on pages 45–47, imagining a white sphere of protective light surrounding you. Take a moment to sit with this energy, asking the Universe and whatever deities, angels or beings you work with for their protection, safe travels and compassion.

Step 3: Making the sigil.

With your pen and paper, write out your statement of intention or what you hope this spell will bring. It's best to begin a statement with phrases such as "I wish" or "It is my will," for example:

> *"It is my will to move through my day safely, with ease and protection."*
>
> *"I wish for travel that is safe, effortless and enjoyable."*
>
> *"This is my wish to move through my day safely, easily and comfortably."*

Once you have your statement, cross out any repeating letters. Then, using the letters that remain, combine them to create a symbol. This symbol is supposed to look weird and not like the actual letters it's made from. Your subconscious mind will attach to this symbol, allowing your conscious mind to forget about the words behind it. Then the magick is able to manifest. You can also make multiple sigils for each part of your intention and combine these into one greater sigil.

Step 4: Charge the sigil.

Once you have your symbol, it's time to infuse it with energy, or charge it. This is like raising a cone of power for the symbol. Keeping the symbol in your mind's eye, or placed physically in front of you, raise the energy, infusing this into the symbol. Once you hit the peak of your energy raising by dancing, chanting or masturbating, look directly at your symbol to help charge it.

Step 5: Draw the sigil.

Using your marker, draw the sigil on whatever pair or pairs of shoes you're blessing. You can draw the sigil on the inside or outside of the shoes (making sure the ink dries before placing them on the floor or wearing them). Once you've drawn the sigil, take a second to close your eyes and infuse your shoes with protection. You may also place your hands on the shoes and say something like the following:

> *"I charm these shoes with protection; may they lead me in a safe direction. With the blessing of the Universe, I cast on thee, protect me from point 'A' to infinity."*

Step 6: Visualize.

Once you've physically drawn the sigil on the shoes, visualize yourself moving safely through different areas: your home and neighborhood, and random places both real and imagined. Imagine a white sphere of light protecting you, with golden-white energy seeping out of your shoes.

Step 7: Close the circle and ground.

When you're finished charming your shoes, close the circle and ground your energy. You can press your forehead into the Earth, imagining all the excess energy returning to her.

Wear your shoes whenever you need some extra protection. You can also retouch the sigil if it starts to fade, infusing more protection into the shoes as you do so.

way of the green witch: earth magick

The Earth is the ultimate muse for the witch. She is alive, thriving, growing and evolving much like us. Earth magick centers around Gaia, the Earth embodied as the Great Mother and all the beings that she grows. By working with herbs, nature and our ancestors, we're able to forge a deeper connection to the Earth and to ourselves. This is the way of the witch and the way of the green witch: walking alongside Nature, learning from her, creating magick with her and leaving her in a better place than when we found her.

This chapter will focus on how to work with herbs like mugwort, lavender and roses as allies. You don't have to have a green thumb to work with plants (though it certainly can help). Nowadays, we're able to buy our herbs sustainably and ethically without having to grow them ourselves. That means we have no excuse to not utilize their magick. (While Earth magick can include working with crystals and stones, we'll be looking at these in more detail in Chapter 7.)

You don't even have to know how to cook to utilize Earth magick. Whether you're working with herb sachets (or herbal bags or pillows) to create psychic dreams, a ritual bath for grounding and protection or an herbal essence for an open heart, this sort of magick will serve you in all areas of your life.

herbs that heal

The first witches worked with herbs intimately. These folk practitioners, medicine women and midwives had an extensive knowledge about how to work with plants as spiritual and physical medicines. They helped deliver babies, cure diseases and ward off negative energy with these plants. Their connection to them was sacred. Thankfully, you don't need this level of knowledge or skill to benefit from a relationship with the Earth and her magick. But there is nevertheless a potent form of magick that comes with creating a working relationship with plants and herbs.

grow your own

If you're a natural green witch, or if you just have a green thumb, you may want to grow your own herbs. You can visit a local plant nursery and talk to them about the best ones to grow in your climate and situation, or you can do your research online. Nowadays, there's a variety of ways to grow herbs. Whether you're using hydroponics or growing them outside in a garden or indoors in a pot, you should be able to find something to suit your lifestyle.

If you are growing your herbs, write a blessing for your plants. Talk to them, form a relationship with them and honor their growth as your own. Breathe with them, invite them to flourish and thank them for their magick. Plant crystals in the soil as a blessing and offering (green moss agate is perfect for this); use your period blood as fertilizer (if you bleed); and incorporate your herbs in your cooking and kitchen witchcraft.

If you have a black thumb like me, then don't stress. You can still find ethically grown herbs that will work just as well in your spells, rituals and offerings.

HOW TO MAKE YOUR OWN SAGE SPRAY

You'll need: spring water (fresh or bottled); clear-grain alcohol or vodka; sage essential oil; a mixing bowl; a small dark glass spray bottle. *Optional:* clear quartz, tourmaline, onyx.

In the bowl, mix together 2 parts water to 1 part alcohol and 1 part sage oil. If you wish, add crystals such as clear quartz, tourmaline or onyx to strengthen the protective magick of this spray. Leave under a full Moon to charge. Then remove the crystals if needed before decanting the liquid into the spray bottle. Use the spray to help clear an area of negativity or heavy energy, or during a full Moon, new Moon or sabbat. Can be used when necessary as a substitute for burning sage.

getting to know your herbs

Plants aren't just physical things; they too have their own spirits and energies. Plants are sentient beings like us, although their senses manifest differently. While each witch will have her own beliefs about the nature of plants, many agree that they have spirits and energies with which we can work and form relationships. Once you begin working with specific herbs, you'll start to form your own relationship with them. Suddenly, for example, you may find rosemary starts calling to you when you're energetically depleted, or lavender begins to beckon you when you can't sleep.

Again, the key word is relationship. Your relationship with herbs will be unique to you and, again, that's totally okay! If you want to start working with herbs but don't know where to start, you can refer to the alphabetical list below for some accessible and powerful plant materials to get you started. (Strictly speaking, herbs tend to come from the leafy green part of the plant, while spices can come from the root, stem, flower or bark.) When it comes to herbs associated with love, most will work for any kind of love, whether it's romantic, familial or friendly. Red roses are generally great for romantic and sexual love, while lavender is good for attracting all kinds of love as well as healing heartache. However, it's your intention while working with these plant materials that will make all the difference.

BAY LEAF

Used by priestesses in Ancient Greece to help them channel the Oracle of Delphi, bay is a multipurpose herb that helps to ward off negative energy and offer protection, as well as attract love. Thanks to this plant's protective properties, you can use bay leaves to clear the energy in your home. According to myth, a crown of bay leaves was worn by the very first Olympians, and they can still be given as gifts at rituals of initiation. Burn bay leaves to help induce a vision, and place them under your pillow for inspiration and psychic dreams.

Try: burn bay leaves as an offering to any deities you work with. You can also scatter the ashes on the floor in a purification ritual, or scatter the leaves and sweep them out the door as a protective ritual.

CINNAMON

One of the easiest spices to access, cinnamon can help to protect, ground and cleanse. It increases focus as well as good fortune, and can be worn in a talisman or amulet. Cinnamon bark is associated with the Lovers tarot card and, when combined with the power of tourmaline, makes for a potent way to consecrate and cleanse ritual items. Cinnamon is associated with the Sun, and can also be used for love and sex magick because of its bright, spicy energy. It can be used for spells around prosperity and abundance, and to enhance psychic abilities, especially when channeling energies.

Try: burn cinnamon before a ritual to cleanse and purify a space.

CORNFLOWER

With its striking bright blue color, cornflower is as beautiful as it is useful. Part of the daisy family, cornflower can be used in matters of the heart, including attracting love. There's a tale that sprinkling cornflower on your right shoe (as opposed to the left) will attract a mate. It is also said to work with the third eye, helping us see the realm of faery. You can work with the flowers by drinking a tea made from it; making it into an eye mask for clairvoyance; sprinkling in a ritual bath to attract love and strengthen your psychic abilities; or using it in spells or offerings.

Try: make an ink from cornflower for use in your grimoire. Boil two cups of fresh flowers (or one cup of dried plant material) in two cups of water in a non-metal container for twenty to thirty minutes. Then strain the liquid into a jar and add two to three drops of vinegar and a pinch of salt to preserve it. Keep it in a dark place and use with a quill to write.

DANDELION

Dandelion is a multipurpose herb, tied to the Greek goddess Hecate and therefore associated with necromancy and the Underworld. A mercurial herb associated with the Element of Air, dandelion can be used to communicate with the dead. Drinking an infusion of dandelion before a ritual is similarly said to help increase psychic abilities and communication with other realms. You can use the roots to make a tea or make wine from the flowers, and then use this in offerings to Hecate. Dandelion is also an excellent herb to incorporate into your diet. Washed and prepared in a salad, the leaves help the function of the gallbladder and liver, and are naturally detoxifying.

Try: turn dandelion roots into a tea. To make the tea, chop up the roots and spread them on a baking sheet. Place in the oven at 475°F, for about two hours. Then grind the roots up in a coffee grinder, before brewing one or two teaspoons of them like coffee or steeping them in a tea bag. While remembering that dandelion is a diuretic, drink as much as you like, but leave a little so when you're done you can go outside and dig a hole, pour some in and walk away without looking back—as an offering to the Greek deities of the Underworld.

LAVENDER

One of the most healing of herbs, lavender can be used to calm anxiety, insomnia and restlessness, and even help with digestive issues. The purple flower and its scent have a calming and sedative effect, and lavender has even been used to treat and disinfect wounds. Lavender can also be used to help with psychic development and protection, as well as to attract love. Put lavender in a pouch under your pillow to aid sleep, hang stalks of it in your bedroom to attract love and burn it during meditation to help open your mind. Part of the mint family, lavender can be used in teas, tonics, baths, and spells and rituals that revolve around healing and/or love.

Try: add lavender to a salt bath for a healing, grounding and calming effect.

MINT

There are a number of uses for mint in all its varieties. And the myth of mint is just as interesting as the leaf itself. The Greek goddess Persephone was jealous of her husband Hades, who set his eye on the water nymph Minthe; so Persephone changed Minthe into a mint plant. Burning mint before bed is supposed to induce prophetic dreams, and mint tea is said to help induce psychic visions. Mint is a protective herb that can be used in healing spells and magick, and to celebrate and invoke success. Mint, thanks to its bright green color, is also a good choice to use for abundance and money magick.

Try: bless your mint before incorporating it in your food or drink. Hold the leaves in your left hand with your right hand placed on top of the mint, and then imagine the energy of protection, abundance or success fusing into the plant. Thank the plant and enjoy it in lemonade, tea, soup or salad.

MUGWORT

Mugwort is a very popular magickal herb that any witch can utilize. Associated with the Moon tarot card, this herb is most often used to enhance dreams. The botanical name of the plant is *Artemisia vulgaris*, after Artemis, the Greek goddess of the hunt, the forest and fertility. Mugwort oil can be used to consecrate ritual items like an athame, as well as to ward off negative energy. Mugwort's connection to the Moon means it opens the channel to the Divine Feminine, the Universe and our psychic senses. You can use mugwort in a smudge stick, in a pillow or as a tea to encourage lucid dreams. When added to amulets or pouches, it assists the safe return of loved ones. You can also rub fresh mugwort leaves on crystal balls and scrying mirrors to help increase their powers.

Try: put a sprig of mugwort in your shoe to help combat fatigue on long journeys.

ROSE

Everyone knows the rose, one of the most beloved flowers
of all. The flower of Aphrodite, the Greek goddess of
love, beauty and sex, the rose is a symbol of love, healing
and hope. Roses represent the ability to love and nurture,
encouraging the heart to grow and blossom. This flower helps
stimulate joy as well as pleasure. Roses are excellent to use in
healing matters, specifically concerning the heart and love.
Simply buying roses and placing them in your space is beneficial.
The rose may likewise be used for magick and divination
pertaining to love, and can be used to honor the Goddess in
rituals. With a variety of uses, the rose can be used in oils for the
skin and hair, in ointments and in rose water.

Try: make some rose water. Take the petals of six or seven organic
roses, place these in a pot and add enough distilled or spring water
to cover them. On a medium-low heat, bring the petals to a
simmer and cover with a lid for twenty to thirty minutes, until the
petals have lost their color. Strain the mixture and pour the liquid
into a glass jar. Decant this mixture into a spray bottle, then shake
it and use it on your skin or to cleanse your altar, mirror or ritual
tools—or pretty much whatever you like.

ROSEMARY

A resilient and fragrant herb, rosemary has traditionally been
used on important occasions such as funerals and weddings, and
as decorations for sabbats. Utilizing rosemary during important
events helps make the occasion more sacred, while also
facilitating a better memory of the event. In Sicily, legend has it
that faeries live in rosemary and are able to shapeshift into small

snakes. Rosemary is also a very cleansing and protective herb, helping ground us while keeping away negativity and malevolence. Rosemary can be used for rituals and spells of love, fidelity and remembrance. It can be used in ritual baths, in kitchen witchcraft as a seasoning or as a perfume.

Try: wear rosemary oil or perfume to an interview so the employer remembers you.

VERVAIN

Also known as verbena, vervain was one of the sacred herbs for many ancient peoples, including the Celts, Greeks, Romans and Welsh. This probably has to do with the array of uses for the herb, including the fact that it can empower any magick. You can use vervain to cleanse and consecrate altar tools, to protect someone from negative emotions, to aid in dream quests and even to help bless and cleanse a space. You can also work with this herb to help find true love, to attract a mate or lover and to work sex magick. Associated with the Roman goddess Diana, this herb can be worn by itself as an amulet, added to spell jars, made into sachets and incorporated in cooking.

Try: make a sachet of vervain for clairvoyant and lucid dreams. Using red thread, sew a pouch of silver fabric measuring between four by four to six by six inches long. Put dried vervain, mugwort and marigold in it for prophetic dreams. Place it above your headboard or under your pillow.

AN HERBAL ELIXIR FOR AN OPEN HEART

Elixirs are a form of tincture: a mixture made from alcohol and herbs, only with added honey or sweetener. Hawthorn, apple and rose are all from the same family, and along with honey, all promote an open heart, so this quick, herbal pick-me-up is for whenever you want to channel and open your own heart.

You'll need: a glass jar (a standard jam jar would be perfect); 80 percent proof alcohol (vodka works great and other spirits will do, although the clearer the better); liquid sweetener (for example, runny honey, glycerine, maple syrup, simple syrup or agave); one tablespoon each of the following dried herbs: hawthorn leaf and flower, organic rose, apple, cinnamon, chamomile (pick as many different herbs as you like, but material from three to five types is usually a sweet spot); muslin or cheesecloth to strain the mixture; small amber dropper bottle(s); tape and a permanent marker to label.

Step 1: Prepare the herbs and add the alcohol and sweetener.

Using a coffee grinder or a blender, finely chop your herbs of choice. Place the herbs in the jar. Then cover with 2 parts alcohol and 1 part sweetener. (If you use fresh herbs or flowers, add a little bit more alcohol. To have a shelf life, a liquid must be 20 percent alcohol. With the sugar, the preservative qualities are even higher.) Label the jar with the date, herbs and alcohol used.

Step 2: Store in a cool dark place.

Store the jar in a cool, dark place like a closet or a pantry for two to three weeks. Making sure the lid is firmly closed, shake the liquid several times a week.

Step 3: Strain.

After the elixir has been sitting for at least two weeks, it's time to strain it. You can either strain it into a measuring cup or straight into the amber dropper bottles. (Not only do the bottles make great holiday gifts, they are also good for storing individual quantities of the elixir.) Cover the mouth of the jar containing the elixir with the cheesecloth or muslin, and then strain. Once all the herbal matter is in the cloth, make sure to squeeze it over the cup or bottle to get any extra liquid out. Then pour the elixir into the amber bottles. (A funnel may help.)

Step 4: Label the bottles and enjoy!

Label the bottles with the date, herbs and alcohol used. Take half a teaspoon of elixir as needed and enjoy! You can add this to water, drinks or simply take as is whenever you need some extra connection to your heart.

other ways to work with herbs

There are a number of ways to work with herbs. As we've seen, you can incorporate them in your cooking, in your skincare routine, in your daily ritual practice, in your spells and more. Making herbal teas, tinctures and elixirs, ritual baths, essences and waters are a few easy, inexpensive and accessible ways to work directly with the energy of the Earth and whichever herbs you choose.

A word of caution: before you work with any herb, it's important to research it to make sure it won't harm you, since there are herbs that are poisonous, like hemlock and lily of the valley.

TEAS

Who doesn't enjoy drinking tea? The warm liquid is comforting, and the aroma is healing in itself. Whether you're creating a ritual out of drinking your tea or simply taking a few minutes to enjoy the cup, it's a powerful remedy and potent way to see and feel the healing effect of herbs.

A SIMPLE TEA RITUAL TO EASE ANXIETY AND STRESS

When you are feeling anxious and stressed, I recommend preparing and drinking a tea made from organic dried herbs, consisting of 1 part lavender, chamomile or mint to 3 parts rose hips, lemon balm and valerian.

HERBS FOR PROTECTION

Every day, our energy mingles with that of the world around us. The beings in the natural world, astral world and physical world all have an impact on our bodies and spirits. Protection magick is its own realm of work that has been utilized by every culture in some form or another. And while there's no right way to work with protection magick, one way that might appeal to the green witch is to work with protective herbs, specifically through sachets. A sachet is a bag of herbs that can be placed somewhere particular or carried for protection. By using herbs that ward off negativity, heal and protect, you can ensure that the Earth is giving you some extra TLC and protection as you go about your daily life.

A SACHET FOR PROTECTION

This sachet uses protective herbs and a banishing charm to keep a particular area—whether it's a home or car—safe and protected. This charm is best done at the full, waxing or new Moon.

You'll need: a white cotton cloth or purple velvet fabric (make sure it's not too thick to gather the edges together) that is about seven inches square in size; red string; a red candle; three or five of the following herbs: rosemary, rue, basil, vervain, mugwort, mistletoe, St. John's wort; any protective stones such as labradorite, onyx and tourmaline.

Step 1: Cleanse your space and ground.

Take a moment to cleanse your space; burning sage and frankincense would be great for this. With all your supplies ready at hand, ground and center yourself. Connect to the Earth and her power. Decide which space you'd like to protect before beginning the next step.

Step 2: Create the sachet.

Once you're done grounding, place all the herbs in the center of your fabric. Imagine them infused with white light; then gather up the edges, wrap the red thread around them and firmly tie together. Make a knot and say:

"I banish negativity, and create a safe space for thee."

Tie four more knots, one for each Element, saying:

"May this sachet guard and protect this [the space you're protecting] and all who find themselves in it."

Step 3: Charge it with the candle.

Once you've said your charm, place the sachet on your altar in front of the red candle. Imagine the white light from earlier growing from the sachet and encompassing you. Light the red candle and visualize your sachet forming a protective bubble around whatever it is you're protecting. Hold this protection as truth in your heart. Then say:

"I create this boundary of protection,
I install this boundary of protection,
I maintain this boundary of protection,
That negative energy shall never find its way in.
So it is."

Let the candle burn all the way down.

Step 4: Ground the energy.

Once your candle is burned and your spell is done, take a moment to ground your energy, feeling that same protection and connection you did before. Press your forehead into the floor, imagining all the excess energy moving back into the Earth.

Step 5: Hang up the sachet.

Once you're done charging it, hang the sachet above the main entrance to your home or in your closet. You can also keep it under the driver's seat of your car or hidden in whatever space you're protecting.

ritual baths

One of my favorite ways to work with herbs is by taking ritual baths. These don't have to be long and complicated, but they can be tailored to your needs and tastes. Before performing rituals or rites, taking a bath of purification is common, often using herbs such as basil, hyssop, mugwort, rosemary and rue, or a combination of these, to help cleanse the body and the energetic field. And while there can be a whole ritual around taking a ritual bath, the act of soaking in the tub and not doing anything else can be an act of magick in itself. Grab candles that correspond to your magickal intention or simply stick to silver, black and white for protection, cleansing and healing. The following ritual herbal bath is great for self-care, and for rejuvenating spirit and soul, especially after heartache.

A RITUAL BATH FOR SELF-LOVE AND HEALING

This simple ritual bath utilizes a few easy-to-access herbs to help heal and cleanse, while also attracting love. This ritual can be done any time, but is best done on a Friday (see the Tables of Correspondences on pages 274–77) and during a full or waxing Moon.

You'll need: Epsom salts; sage or palo santo; a bathtub; herbs like organic rose petals, lavender, calamint, lemon balm, cornflower or any combination of these. Optional: pink or white candles; rose quartz, clear quartz and amethyst; rose and lavender essential oils; anything else you need to make yourself feel comfortable and relaxed.

Step 1: Cleanse yourself and prepare.

Cleanse yourself by carefully smudging around your body with palo santo or sage. If you wish, you can also cleanse your bathroom and tub. Put on some music, light some incense and take a few deep breaths.

Step 2: Draw your ritual bath.

Run the bath and place the herbs in the tub, scattering rose petals on the surface. Step into the bath, being mindful of the temperature, while continuing to connect to your breath. Lie back and focus on the connection to your sacral chakra and your heart. Then say:

"I am love. I am open to love. I accept an abundance of love. I am worthy of love."

You can also write your own affirmations and say them. Then dunk your head under the water as a ritual of cleansing. Now enjoy your bath. Breathe, relax, meditate and feel the herbs heal you.

Step 3: Finish the ritual.

When you're ready, blow out any candles, drain the water and slowly start to dry yourself off. You can spray some rose spray on your skin or put on your favorite lotion.

You may adapt this template for whatever ritual bath you're doing, using herbs that correspond to your intention. Play around with different affirmations, and enjoy the healing powers of the water.

the kitchen witch

If you love or even just like to cook, why not incorporate some magick into your kitchen? You can bless your food as you cook it; use condiments to draw banishing or invoking pentagrams and sigils; use herbs with specific correspondences in your cooking (like rosemary and sage for protection, mint for money, etc.); and infuse your food with gratitude before you cook it. Display your herbs in decorative jars (but not in direct sunlight, so your herbs stay potent), clean your counters with Florida or herbal water and turn your kitchen into a sacred space.

Start thinking of meals as a form of spellwork: the preparation can be your grounding, the cooking is raising the energy, and eating like releasing the cone of power. Again, find what feels best for you and go from there.

nature
spirits

It doesn't matter whether you live in a city, a suburb or the countryside: there's Nature all around you; sometimes you just have to look. Taking a Nature walk can be like a walking meditation that invites you to explore the fauna and flora around you.

To go for a Nature walk, put your phone on silent and find an area you can walk around safely. Look around you; notice any plants, trees, bushes or wildflowers. See if there's anything that catches your eye and explore this. Keep an eye out for any wildlife that might make itself known. Notice the color of the sky, the feeling of the wind, the shape of the leaves on the trees. See how present you can be. Take a moment to find your breath and register any feelings you have. If you come across any flowers, nuts, pine cones, shells or other natural items—and if it's okay to do so—collect these gifts and perhaps use them in rituals later on, or simply place them on your altar. When you're back home, thank the Earth for all you've learned.

Besides plants and wildlife, you might find that spending time in Nature helps you to connect with other, ancient energies such as faeries, sylphs and undines.

the faery folk

The faery folk have existed since the dawn of time in every corner of the globe. They are the natural world incarnate. They are the energy of the trees, the whisper of the flowers, the cause of that mischievous cat seemingly chasing nothing. The faery folk—also known as faeries, fairies, the little people and the fey—are the true ancestors of Nature. They are the beings that inhabit the natural world. They exist in the astral realm, although they do cross over to our world from time to time. At the Equinoxes, at Midsummer, on Halloween and whenever the veil thins between our world and theirs, they can come visit us in our realm.

The term "faery" works as an umbrella term for various magickal beings that live on the astral plane. Nymphs, unicorns, mermaids, salamanders, dragons and more all fall under the domain of the faery. Just like there are different types of animals and people, there are different types of faeries, each with their own distinct spirit. Though their existence has been disputed for centuries, to believe in faeries is to see them. To acknowledge their presence is to acknowledge the beauty of the natural world, and the spirit that keeps her alive. Faery sightings in our realm are rare, but the more you work with them, the more you'll sense their energy and their presence. And, who knows, maybe one day you'll have your own faery sighting as well.

WHAT TO REMEMBER WHEN WORKING WITH FAERIES

There are a few ground rules for working with the faery. If you're going to a natural space, make sure not to leave any litter. Clean up the space, leaving it in better shape than you found it. And always leave an offering when you work with the fey. This can be cake, fruit, wine, sweets, honey or milk. But don't say thank you. This causes offense to them; instead, feel the energy of gratitude before leaving your offering.

Many times, the faeries will give you something in return for your offering, like a beautiful stone or stick. If something catches your eye after you leave your offering, take it. You may incorporate this into your magick or place it upon your altar.

Don't ring bells before working with them, as it's said to scare them. And don't wear or work with iron either, as this is said to repel them.

types of faery

There are way too many types of faery to list all of them, so instead we're going to focus on a faery for each Element. These entities embody the energy of their respective Element, yet they are still their own beings and shouldn't be lumped into any categories.

EARTH: GNOME

Gnomes look rather like you'd expect them to: quite elderly since they age fast, although they're believed to live to be about 1,000 years old. These creatures of the Earth are said to live in the root systems of ancient oak trees, where they focus on helping to heal wildlife and animals. The reason we have ornamental gnomes can be traced to these beings, as placing their effigies in our yards and gardens can help bless and protect these spaces. The energy of the gnome, which relates to the North and therefore the Element of the Earth, may be called upon during a ritual or spell to protect you and your pets. They also lend themselves to healing spells, and can help teach the secrets of herbalism. And since they love to dance, you may ask the gnomes to help you raise energy during a ritual by this method; if you're honoring a deity of the forest, they'll be even more inclined to help.

How to connect to the gnomes: meditate at the base of an old oak tree, either in real life or by visualizing this in the astral realm. If the latter, you can either imagine visiting a familiar tree, or make one up. Close your eyes, ground and connect to the tree. Feel its presence and wisdom before asking to connect with the gnomes. Nothing may happen the first time, so be patient and take your time. When you've finished meditating, leave them an offering. This can be milk, honey, bread or something sweet. Invite them to dance with you when you're next raising energy during a healing or protection spell. Ask them to protect your pets, and leave offerings for them at the base of old oak trees.

AIR: SYLPH

Thought to originate in Greece and Egypt, sylphs appear as small, winged creatures. Given their ethereal nature, their wings might not even be necessary for them to fly. These beings may be called upon for work of all kinds—though anything relating to the Element of Air and its corresponding direction, the East, is especially appropriate. Air represents our inspiration, our wishes and desires, and in the same way, the sylphs rule over these areas too. When we play, when we laugh, when we love, when we find expansion and growth and space; this is the realm of the sylph.

How to connect to the sylphs: you can invoke the sylphs during a ritual when you're calling in the Element of Air. Turn to face the East and ask the sylphs to join you, opening your heart to them. You can also do this simple ritual: take a second to ground, feeling the Earth supporting you. Then sense the air above, and start connecting to that Element. Acknowledge the presence of the sylphs and invite them to join you. Next, create a piece of art inspired by them: draw, paint, color, sew, write, sketch or do whatever else pleases you creatively. During the process of creating your art, remain aware of that connection to the Element of Air. When you've finished, place the artwork on your altar and light a yellow candle. Then meditate or dance, once more calling on the energy of the sylphs. When you're ready, ground your energy. Finally, leave an offering for the sylphs on your altar or outside.

FIRE: SALAMANDER

Salamanders are the energetic equivalent of the lizards with the same name. Rulers of Fire and the direction of the South, the salamander is a being you can call upon for an extra dose of fire and passion. But if they're around too long they can become disruptive, so it's best to banish these beings once their work is done. Salamanders can be invoked for protection magick, where their heat and fiery spirits can be utilized in full force. If you're working with these beings, do be careful. If you're burning something during a ritual where you've called upon them, scatter the ashes somewhere outside. You can also banish them directly, saying: "I banish thee, salamanders, back to the realm of the faery."

How to connect with salamanders: an easy and safe way to work with these beings is to do a fire gazing. This is pretty much what it

IT DOESN'T
MATTER WHETHER
YOU LIVE IN THE
CITY, A SUBURB
OR THE COUNTRY:
THERE'S NATURE
ALL AROUND YOU,
YOU JUST HAVE
TO LOOK.

sounds like. Although you can use any candle to do this exercise, one that's red or orange would work exceptionally well. As always, take a second to ground and connect, feeling the Earth supporting you. Invite the energies of the salamanders in, asking them for protection, for light or just to be there. Once you're ready, open your eyes and light your candle. Take a comfortable seat with the flame placed in front of you, and gaze at it, relaxing your eyes without letting them cross. Start breathing rhythmically, keeping your gaze on the flame of the candle. Do you feel or see anything? Be patient. You may not register anything, but you can keep coming back to this. Snuff out the candle when you're done by using a candle snuffer or a fan. You can use the same candle whenever you do this meditation. When you're done with the gazing say: "I banish thee, salamanders, back to the realm of the faery," before grounding your energy and leaving them an offering of milk, honey, wine or sweets.

WATER: UNDINE

Associated with the Element of Water and the West, undines are said to look like a few different things; some see them as seahorses with human faces, some regard them as looking more like women. The word "undine" is an umbrella term of sorts for beings that include mermaids and the Nereids, which are nymphs of the sea. Their abode is in the ocean and in bodies of water, especially if these are natural and located far away from civilization. The undine's connection to the Element of Water relates to our connection to our emotions, to the feminine aspect of our soul and to the fluid, effortless nature of being that is found in both ourselves and the ocean. You may call upon the undines to enhance the magick of any spell or ritual, although this will be especially potent if working with the Element of Water, or anything pertaining to the emotions and healing.

How to connect with undines: find a body of water either in the physical realm or on the astral plane by visualizing it. (You can also do this exercise in the bath.) Ground your energy, connecting with the power of the Earth beneath you. If you can, go into the water, and start singing. Swim if you're able, before floating on your back. Breathe into the water, feeling her support. Imagine the undines carrying and supporting you. Feel them holding your body and filling it with white light. If you need some healing, tell them about what's going on and ask for their help. Breathe into your heart space, imagining a white light, and notice if you see or feel anything different. Once you feel like your time is complete, leave the water. Ground your energy, leave an offering and be on your way.

CHAPTER SIX

the moon as muse: moon magick

Witchcraft is riddled with folklore about the Moon. During sabbats, usually when the Moon was full, witches would gather in fields and honor the Moon as the Great Mother by dancing, chanting and raising energy. The Moon was worshipped as the Roman goddess Diana, as the Aztec goddess Coyolxauhqui, as the Greek goddess Selene. The Moon touches us in a special way; a reminder from the heavens that no matter what happens there's always a light.

Even today, ask nearly any witch about the Moon and she's sure to gush. The Moon is our muse, our mother, our goddess, our creatrix. Her light illuminates the darkness and our soul. Her craters reflect our depths. Her ebb and flow reflects our own, reminding us of the cycles we go through every month. And for those of us who bleed, the Moon reminds us of the way we grow, die and transform each month, just like the Moon as she waxes and wanes.

The Moon represents our inner world. While the Sun illuminates our truth, our passions and our light, the Moon rests her gaze on the realm of the subconscious. Her whispers are more subtle; caresses on flesh, flashes of insight in our mind's eye, the whispering of truths in our ear as we contemplate her silky surface. She is the subtle energy of the Universe personified; she is one of the greatest teachers we have, and a reminder that we're allowed to transform as often as we like.

In the tarot, the Moon is a double truth. On the one hand, she represents our inner darkness—our subconscious mind, the dream world, our shadows and whatever hides in the darkness. She tells us of our shame, of what we bury under layers of ink so black that we don't have to see it anymore. But the Moon wouldn't have light if she weren't reflecting the Sun; and this is the other face of her duality. In this way, the Moon lights up our shadow. She invites us to explore our inner realm, to dive into the ocean of our soul. When we track our own energy next to that of the Moon, we're tapping into the way our ancestors tracked their life and growth as well. Not only is this natural, it's easy too.

sympathetic moon magick

I talked a little bit about sympathetic magick earlier in this book, in Chapter 1, but in my opinion one of the easiest ways to work with this practice is with the Moon. Sympathetic magick is a form of magick that imitates its desired outcome. A staged hunt with the outcome that is hoped for in the real hunt and working with the Moon's phases are examples of this.

Each month, we enjoy a fresh energetic slate thanks to the new Moon. This is when the Moon's in her darkest phase, when no light is reflected back at us and she's inky black like a scrying mirror. As her light starts to wax, or grow, until it reaches its apex at the full Moon, we can perform magick concerning what we want to manifest. As the Moon's light grows, *we* grow too; and we focus our magick around this during the new Moon, waxing Moon and full Moon. When the Moon is at her fullest, this is a powerful time to focus on any sort of magick we want to (although banishing spells are best saved for the waning or new Moon). As the Moon's light wanes, or loses light, we work magick on whatever we want to release, let go of or banish from our lives. And then at the next new Moon, the cycle starts all over again.

In the West, our calendars are run by the Sun and its reign. But I would argue that our bodies are naturally more connected with the Moon. If the Moon controls the tides, and our bodies are over 70 percent water, it makes sense that we feel her effects too. By working alongside her lunar rhythms, we have an easy and potent form of magick that will be there for us month after month. And, as we have seen, each phase of the Moon's journey has its own specific medicine that we can use and tap into whenever we need. Having some basic background information about each phase will allow you to access and harness the Moon's energy to enhance your spells, ritual, magick and energy work.

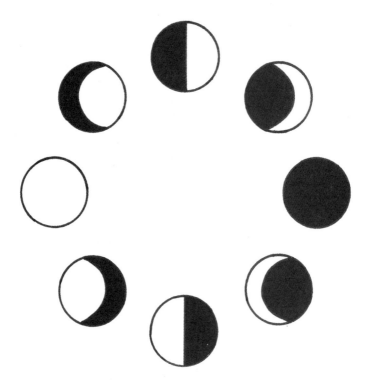

new moon

The new Moon is like a fresh page in a notebook, like a clean slate, like waking up after a long nap ready for what the day holds. It's the start of a new energetic cycle, and it's the day when we're able to dive the deepest into our shadows and the abyss of our hearts and souls. The new Moon, also known as the dark Moon, is when we set our eyes on the month ahead. The power of the new Moon is strongest on the actual day (often marked in calendars as a black dot), and potent for two and a half days before and after this.

The new Moon is a great time to plant seeds and set goals. You can create a monthly ritual out of this lunar phase by reading your tarot cards, looking at your spiritual, physical and mental health and life, and figuring out where you need more support. Even if there's nothing new you need to plant, there may be something that needs nurturing from previous months or seasons.

The new Moon is also a time when we can banish whatever no longer serves us. While this work can be done during the waning Moon as well, banishing negative energy or binding negative energy (to release or tie up, respectively) is also supported in the darkest phase of the Moon. You can perform the binding spell on page 208, or start it on the waning Moon and then finish it at the new Moon.

Journaling prompts for the new Moon: What is it that I intend to grow and feed during this Moon cycle? What do I need more of in my life to feel fulfilled? What steps can I take to cultivate new or existing passions? Try writing a list of goals of what you want to accomplish in the next month.

A SIMPLE SPELL FOR MANIFESTATION

You'll need: a white pillar candle (or a color that corresponds to whatever you want to manifest; see below and the section on Candle Magick 101 in Chapter 8); a piece of paper and pen; a toothpick. *Optional*: any oils, herbs and crystals associated with your goal.

» *Money/Abundance*: a green candle, cinnamon, ginger or patchouli oil.

» *Love*: a pink candle, rose petals, ylang-ylang or jasmine oil.

» *Health*: a white candle, eucalyptus, cypress or coriander oil.

» *Creativity*: an orange candle, peppermint, clary sage or tangerine oil.

Step 1: Ground, center and cast your circle.

Ground your energy, finding the space at the base of your spine where the Earth supports you. Breathe into this, feeling the connection to the Earth grow stronger and stronger. Cast your circle by walking around your space clockwise while pointing your finger, a wand or athame and imagining a sphere of white protective energy forming around you.

Step 2: Write your intention and dress your candle.

Write your intention, or petition, on a piece of paper. Then write a sentence or a few words on your candle about what you want to manifest. Use a toothpick, pin or a needle to carve this into the candle, from the bottom to the top. If you're dressing your candle with herbs and oils, now's the time to do so. Using your oil of choice, put some in your hands and cover the candle with it, moving from the top to the middle and then from the bottom to the middle, which is the way you attract in candle magick. Then place the herbs atop the oil in the same manner, making sure to cover each side of the candle.

Step 3: Call it in.

Once you've dressed your candle, reconnect with your breath and then light the candle. Really feel what you want; what would it be like to receive what you're asking for? Hold this in your heart as you read from your paper to the candle, asking the Universe, your guides, angels or deities for their support and compassion concerning what you wish to manifest. Declare your intention, then place the paper near the candle (or you can burn it if you prefer). Light this candle every day up until the full Moon if you can, repeating your intention. If you finish before the full Moon, that's okay too, but on the full Moon, bury the wax and paper at a crossroads or dispose of them at an intersection.

Step 4: Ground and release.

Once you've declared what you want, take a moment to sit and connect with it. When you're ready, use a fan, a lid or a candle snuffer to put out the candle (but don't blow it out). Close your circle, using whatever you used before while walking around it counterclockwise. Press your forehead to the floor and release any excess energy back into the Earth.

waxing moon

The waxing Moon falls between the new and full Moon, with the first quarter Moon falling a week after the new Moon and a week before the full. This is like a stop on the train when we can get off, explore and check where we're going. It's when we can examine our inventory, get back on track and make sure we're on the way to where we want to be. You can focus on manifesting magick during this phase, or you can use it to continue any spells or work that you may have started during the new Moon.

The waxing Moon is a good time to try out new things too. Unlike the full Moon, which can be intense energetically, the waxing Moon is the perfect time to go on a blind date, try a new class, learn a new skill or create something. You can use this time to perform magick, to check in or to challenge yourself. You can even do none of this and just take it as a week in which to nurture yourself with whatever it is that you need in the moment; again, there's no wrong way to practice. Being honest about your progress and tweaking anything necessary to make this more seamless is a good way to work with this energy as well.

Journal prompts for the waxing Moon: What stage have I reached in pursuit of the goals I set at the new Moon, and what still needs work? What have I nurtured since the new Moon, and what must I continue to nurture? What's been calling to me that I've been ignoring? Where do I need more passion?

A SPELL FOR SELF-CARE AND SELF-LOVE

This spell is best performed on a Friday or Monday (see the Tables of Correspondences on pages 274–77).

You'll need: a bath (although you can use a shower); rose quartz; a mirror (preferably full length); and a pink candle. *Optional:* rose petals, lavender, Epsom salts.

Step 1: Take a ritual bath.

Make sure your phone is off and that you'll be undisturbed. If you wish, play some ambient or relaxing music. Fill your tub with warm water and, if using, add the Epsom salts. Standing at the edge of your tub, take a few deep breaths. Sprinkle the rose petals and the lavender onto the water. Step into the tub, continuing to be led by your breath, taking as much time as you need to soak, relax and center. Use this bath as a way to ground. (See also the bath ritual for self-love and healing on pages 182–83.)

Step 2: Mirror affirmations.

Step out of the tub, dry yourself off and apply any lotions, oils or perfumes that make you feel luxurious and beautiful (rose or jasmine would be an excellent choice). Then find your way to a mirror. Start to connect with your heart, breathing into this space and holding the light there, imagining a warm ball glowing larger and larger, enveloping you. Take your rose quartz and hold it in your left hand and say:

"I am love. I am open to love. I am receptive of love. I am abundant with love."

Step 3: Light the candle.

Once you feel ready, move to your altar. Hold the rose quartz in your left hand as you light the pink candle with your right. Repeat the affirmation. Let the candle burn all the way down if you can. If you can't let it burn down, light it every night until the full Moon. Then dispose of the wax by burying it at a crossroads, or disposing of it in a trash can at an intersection.

Step 4: Ground and center.

Once the candle has been extinguished or burned down, take a deep breath and exhale noisily through your mouth. Feel the light in your heart from earlier. Hold this as you press your forehead into the ground and release any excess energy.

full moon

A favorite among the witches, the full Moon is the most energetically potent day of the month. This is when the Moon is illuminated in all her glory, reflecting back to us our hidden layers as she uncovers each one a little more. The full Moon tends to intensify everything, which means this is not an ideal time to try new things. Each full Moon carries a specific energy, depending on which astrological sign both the Moon and the Sun are in. But the power is usually the same; it's strong, it's juicy, it's full, and more than anything it asks what we want and need. This is a day when we can look back at the new

THE MOON
LIGHTS UP OUR
DARKNESS. SHE
INVITES US TO
EXPLORE OUR
INNER REALM, TO
DIVE INTO THE
OCEAN OF OUR
SOUL.

Moon and really see our growth and achievements since then. The full Moon is also a time of increased psychic ability, so you may be sensing things extra strongly. Any magick work can be performed at this time, including manifestations, love and prosperity magick, healing, divination and psychic work. After the full Moon, the light starts to wane, which means we focus on what we want to release.

An easy way to connect with the power of this phase is to sit under the Moon's rays and gaze at her. Spend at least five minutes, if you can, gazing at her surface, breathing and connecting to her light.

A Supermoon occurs when a new or full Moon is at its perigee, or closest point to the Earth in its monthly orbit. During a Supermoon, the Moon can look 14 percent larger and 40 percent brighter than usual. So when we have a Supermoon full Moon, we get extra amplified energy.

Journal prompts for the full Moon: What have I cultivated since the new Moon? What brings me joy? What are my senses and intuition telling me at this time? What's stopping me from showing up as my fullest and truest self?

A SPELL FOR ABUNDANCE AND WEALTH

You'll need: a jar (e.g., an old salsa or pasta jar); honey, sugar, molasses or agave; herbs connected to money such as cinnamon, rosemary, bay leaf, cloves and thyme; jade, malachite or clear quartz; a piece of paper and pen; a green candle. *Optional*: liquor; matches; anything else you want to add to attract money (like a talisman or special coin); sage or palo santo to cleanse.

Step 1: Cleanse your space, ground and center.

Using your herb of choice, cleanse yourself and your space with sacred smoke. Then take a seat, focus on your breath and ground your energy.

Step 2: Cast your circle.

You can either cast your circle as described on pages 45–47, or you can imagine a sphere of energy radiating from your heart, engulfing you and the space you're working in. Breathe into your circle, imagining the protective sphere as impenetrable.

Step 3: Be clear about what you want.

You might pick a specific amount of money you want to attract, or a specific kind of abundance you want to call in (such as emotional, spiritual or physical riches). Once you know what you want, write this on your piece of paper, starting with a phrase such as: "I attract . . . ," "I call in . . . ," or "I receive . . ."

Step 4: Construct the spell.

Fold up your paper and place it in the jar. Start adding herbs, your crystals and whatever else you have, remembering to breathe and connect with your heart. As you add things to your spell jar, know what you're attracting as fact. Add the honey to the jar so everything else is touched by its sweetness.

Step 5: Charge the spell.

Once you've constructed the spell, either melt the bottom of the candle and fix it atop the jar, or place it in front of it. Light the candle and say:

"All this honey [or substitute what you're using], sweet as can be, may you draw abundance and wealth to me."

Then charge the spell and raise the cone of power. You can do this by chanting, dancing, drumming or masturbating. When you feel at the peak of your energy, imagine a cone starting at the base of your circle, moving up into a point and being released into the Universe.

Step 6: Let the candle burn, close the circle and ground the energy.

Once you're done raising the energy, close the circle either by walking around it counterclockwise, as described on page 47, or by drawing the circle back into your heart, down the base of your spine and back into the Earth. Press your forehead into the ground, imagining all the excess energy returning to the Earth.

Let the candle burn all the way down if possible, then dispose of the spell jar by burying it at a crossroads or by putting it in a trash can at an intersection. You can also perform this spell at a new Moon, in which case let the candle burn a little each day up until the full Moon, and then dispose of the jar.

waning moon

During the waning Moon, we get real about what we want to release. What is it that you've been clinging on to this month that you no longer need? Well, the waning Moon is asking you to let that shit go. As the Moon makes her way from full to new again, we have the perfect opportunity to think about what's no longer serving us. Whether it's a negative thought pattern, relationship or even a feeling, we have the opportunity to release this as the Moon's light gets dimmer and dimmer. This is a time to banish, to cast away, to bind, to scream, to yell and to embody, so we can lighten our load once we approach the fresh energy of the new Moon. That said, there may be months when there's nothing you feel like you need to let go of, or maybe you're continuing to work on letting go of something from another month. The waning Moon is when we really see what's holding us back from embodying our full power, when we recognize what's blocking our joy or whatever else we wish to experience. It's a time of decrease, of release, of completion when we are allowed to say "no more" and stand in our power.

A BINDING SPELL FOR A TOXIC OR HARMFUL PERSON

This spell can be used when someone won't respect your boundaries, when they won't listen to you or when you feel like they're abusing your energy. This won't curse them or hex them; instead, this spell works on a subtle level and binds their energy up so they won't be able to use any of it on you.

You'll need: a picture or one of the person's belongings (a lock of hair, sample of handwriting or piece of clothing will also work); a black candle; a lighter or matches; red thread; a pen and paper; water; sage or palo santo, onyx or tourmaline.

Step 1: Ground, center and cast the circle.

Ground your energy, breathing into the base of your spine as you connect to the earth. Imagine energy rising up your spine and into your heart. Then imagine the Cosmos beaming a light into the crown of your head, which moves into your heart, mingling with the energy. Breathe into this power. Using an athame, wand or your finger, walk clockwise as you cast your circle.

Step 2: Call in the Elements.

Call in the Elements, moving clockwise from North around to West, as described on page 41.

Step 3: Focus on your intention—and then bind that shit up.

Keep breathing, finding your connection to the Earth. Be really clear about who or what it is you're binding. Take the photo of the person and write: "I bind [their name]" and then what it is that you're binding them from. This can be as simple as "I bind X from harming anyone," or it can be more specific. If you're using any of this person's belongings, place the item(s) on your altar and write the same thing on the piece of paper. Then, read your petition aloud. You can say something like the following, adapting it to your situation:

"I [your own name] bind [their name]. I bind [their name] in the name of the Universe. I bind [their name] from harming me in the name of the Elements. I bind [their name] by my name. So it is."

Then fold up the piece of paper while imagining the person being caught in a golden lasso they can't get out of; it's strong enough that they can never escape (unless you decide to reverse this spell). Keep focusing on this as you wrap up the piece of paper with the red string. Repeat your petition "I bind [their name]" thirteen times.

Step 4: Light the candle.

Place the crystals around the black candle. Now place your petition in front of this, making sure any items belonging to the person are next to it. Light the candle and repeat what you said before, about binding them by your name and the name of the Universe and the Elements. Once this is said, take a few breaths to connect with your intention. Let the candle burn all the way down, placing it in a sink if you have to.

Step 5: Dismiss the Elements.

Now dismiss the Elements, as described on page 42.

Step 6: Close the circle and ground.

Close the circle with whatever you used to open it. Walk in a counterclockwise direction, feeling the energy moving back into your outstretched hand, up your arm, through your body, back into the Earth. Once you get back to the front of the circle, press your forehead to the ground and imagine any excess energy returning to the Earth.

On the new Moon, bury the wax and the petition at a crossroads, or burn it and flush it down the toilet, or dispose of it at an intersection.

the moon as mother

First things first. God, Goddess, the Universe—whatever it is, it's way bigger than we are. It's so big, so overwhelming, so vast and so powerful that we really can't comprehend it. It's a feeling, a sensation, an energy. But one thing's for sure; it's certainly not human. When we honor a specific goddess or god, we're honoring a slice of the entire pie. We're honoring one aspect of divinity, but we're also honoring a specific entity.

Gods and goddesses have their own divine agenda; they're not all loving or compassionate or understanding, although there are some of them that are. When we start to worship a goddess, we form a relationship with her. We honor her, we serve her, we see her reflected back in us. We leave her offerings, ask for her compassion and we start to create a bond with her.

Many of us in the West grew up worshipping a god. In most major religions, there's no room for a goddess. But the dance of the ancient Goddess, the worship of the Mother, of the Earth, of the Moon—it's an ancient calling we have in our bones. If we're all created in the image of the divine, why is the divine never depicted as feminine? When we work with the Goddess, we're reclaiming our right to matriarchal worship. We're tapping into our past lives, our karma, our history, all carried in our bones. Goddess worship isn't for everyone, but if you feel something stir when you think of honoring the Great Mother or Moon goddess, then it's probably for you.

The Moon is one of the most ancient symbols of our relationship with the Goddess. We personify the Goddess as the Moon, and in the craft, we honor the Moon as the Goddess. When we work with the Moon, we're working with the subtle realm, with our divine darkness, with our power, with our cycles. By working with a goddess who's associated with the Moon, not only are we deepening our relationship to the divine, but we're deepening our relationship to the Moon and the natural world.

moon goddesses of the world

Here are just a few Moon goddesses and goddesses associated with the Moon from different parts of the world. Why not see who catches your (third) eye and work with her?

AUCHIMALGEN—CHILEAN GODDESS AND PROTECTRIX

Auchimalgen is a South American goddess from Chile, who's honored as the Moon. Auchimalgen is a protectrix, keeping us safe from evil and disasters, as well as harmful spirits. She was worshipped by the Araucanian Mapuche people, and was one of their only beneficial deities. Auchimalgen is married to the

Sun, who blesses the Earth with light while she shines through the darkness like a beacon of protection. The colors white and silver, including white flowers and water, are sacred to her. This goddess reminds us that we are protected and loved—and that it is important to see each day as a blessing.

To work with her: wear silver clothing and jewelry; burn lunar incense like jasmine, myrrh or coconut; sprinkle floral water at the entrance of your home to draw Auchimalgen's protective and caring energy to you; place white candles on your altar, and dedicate a piece of silver jewelry to her.

YEMOJA—YORUBAN GODDESS OF THE LIVING OCEAN

Yemoja is a Yoruban orisha, or spirit, and the goddess of the living ocean. She is a source of all the waters, including the rivers in Western Africa. She is where all life begins, and all life is said to be held by her. A motherly and protective goddess, she cares deeply for her children and helps cure our sorrows. In Haitian Voodoo, she is a goddess of the Moon, said to protect mothers and their children. She rules over the state of the ocean, and although she doesn't lose her temper easily, when she does you can expect a violent and destructive storm. Yemoja also rules over the affairs of womanhood, and her soothing and nourishing energy is perfect for rituals surrounding fertility and women's issues. She is said to be the guardian of the collective subconscious and ancient wisdom, since these secrets are held in the ocean. Her reign is over the living ocean, where fish swim and light dances, whereas the orisha Olokun rules over the depths of the ocean. Together, Yemoja and Olokun create balance.

WHEN WE WORK WITH THE MOON, WE'RE WORKING WITH THE SUBTLE REALM, WITH OUR DIVINE DARKNESS, WITH OUR POWER, WITH OUR CYCLES.

To work with her: spend time near the ocean or other bodies of water; sit under the Moon; wear her colors of blue and white. Decorate your altar with blue and white and seashells, blessing it with ocean water in her name.

ISIS—EGYPTIAN GODDESS OF HEALTH, MARRIAGE AND WISDOM

The goddess with a thousand names, Isis was an ancient Egyptian goddess of fertility, motherhood, magick and the Moon, whose name can be interpreted as "Goddess of the Throne." The wife of Osiris and mother of the Sun god Horus, Isis was revered for her ability to help people solve problems through magick. Her cult worshipped her as the "ideal fertile mother" and she is depicted as a woman wearing a vulture-shaped headdress or a crown. Associated with the goddess Hathor, Isis's popularity meant she was the only Egyptian goddess to be worshipped by everyone in the country. While Egyptians worshipped male Moon deities, since Isis is associated with love, fertility and romance, she is also associated with lunar energy. She allows us to feel deeply in relationships, and protects and sustains us. She reminds us of our personal gifts and emotional depths—and that we're always invited to explore this space.

To work with her: wear her colors of silver and white; work with bloodstone or carnelian; wear a *tyet* (knot of Isis) amulet for protection against evil; meditate with her; gaze at the Moon; and ask for her blessing and assistance during magickal work.

KUAN YIN—EAST ASIAN GODDESS OF PRAYERS, WOMEN AND CHILDREN

Technically, Kuan Yin (also spelled Kwan Yin, Quan Yin and Guanyin) is not a goddess. She's actually a bodhisattva. She was destined to become a Buddha, or an "enlightened one," but chose to stay on Earth to answer the prayers of mothers and children, and to save all beings from suffering. She is known for her compassion and mercy, and can be called upon for these qualities and healing and guidance. Kuan Yin is associated with the Moon, serving as a reminder that she's always listening and watching us, ready to offer us compassion, insight and love. A motherly goddess, Kuan Yin is protective, nurturing and loving, much like the energy of the Moon.

To work with her: pray to her; gaze at the Moon; drink black tea in her name and leave it as an offering; decorate your altar with lotus flowers and rainbows; leave sweet cakes and fresh fruit as an offering; and pray to her for blessings, protection and love.

SELENE—GREEK GODDESS OF THE MOON

The sister of the Sun god Helios and of Eos, the goddess of the dawn, Selene is the only Greek deity to be regarded as a personification of the Moon herself. Although she's associated with the goddess Artemis, Selene has a separate identity and is depicted as a woman riding sidesaddle on a horse or in a chariot drawn by winged steers. Worshipped at the new and full Moon, and said to derive power from her Moon chariot, Selene was an important deity for agriculture and played a part in daily rituals. She has control over time, and the power to give sleep as well as to light the night.

To work with her: decorate your altar with images of the Moon; work with moonstone; Moon gaze; wear her colors of silver and white; decorate your altar with white roses and white candles; call upon her at the full Moon and the new Moon.

creating a goddess-based practice

Working with goddesses, or any deity really, is a consistent (and hopefully daily) practice. It's a song that plays in the background as you go about your day. Goddess worship doesn't mean meditating for hours on end and holding yourself back from living. Instead, it's an invitation to form your own deep connection with divinity in a tangible way. Your practice, like your work with witchcraft, isn't going to look like someone else's—and that's totally okay! What matters is your intention and dedication, not to mention love.

An easy way to establish a connection with Goddess energy is to create an altar. This can be dedicated to the Moon or to a specific goddess. Clean and honor this space regularly, and let it serve as the altar of your temple. Meditating with the energy of a goddess, or simply calling out to her before you meditate, is another way to work with her. You can dress in her colors or in her favorite metals or fabrics, burn incense she loves and create your own special connection with her. Go outside every night and try to find the Moon. Talk to her, ask for her compassion and allow yourself to feel connected with her. Leaving offerings is another way to show devotion. Personally, my favorite way to connect with the Goddess is to create in her honor. Make art, write poetry, take photos, create a meal, dance, sing and worship her. Find a connection between you and your chosen goddess, and whatever she rules over. Cast a spell in her honor, invite her energy and compassion in during rituals and carve out a few minutes each day, or as often as you can, to talk to, connect with and worship her.

CHARGING OBJECTS AND TALISMANS BY THE MOON

You can invite in the energy of the Moon by charging your objects with her light. On the night of a full Moon, bring out your crystals, talismans, icons, tarot cards and whatever else you want to charge. The Moon's own energy will help clear and charge these sacred objects, as will the Sun's energy. If you wish, leave your talismans and stones in natural light for twenty-four hours to strengthen their charge (although some stones such as amethyst, citrine, fluorite, rose quartz and smoky quartz shouldn't be left in direct sunlight as they can fade).

Another potent way to work with the energy of the Moon is by charging water with her rays. Fresh or spring water is preferable, but any type will do. You can also put crystals in the water for extra energy; moonstone or any kind of quartz works great. You can use this water to make holy water (see page 272), as well as in spell and ritual work and to call in the Elements.

When you're charging these objects, you can also call upon the Goddess or a specific goddess like Selene or Yemoja for their compassion, blessings and energy.

rhythms of the moon

Those of us who bleed go through an intense cycle each month.
Our bodies get ready to support life, and if they don't have to do
this, they shed their layers. As the Moon's light grows and then
wanes, so do aspects of our bodies. And we can learn about our
bodies depending on when we bleed.

WHITE MOON

Those who bleed when the Moon is new or waning follow what's
called a "white Moon cycle." The Earth is said to be at its most
fertile during the full Moon, which is when those with a white
Moon cycle ovulate. If you bleed at this time, you'll probably have
a stronger sense of intuition now and an urge to recharge, renew
and withdraw so you can find nourishment. Since the new Moon
represents a fresh start, like your period, you have the advantage
of charting your monthly cycle the same way you chart your
goals for the month. Pay attention to your gut feelings and needs
during this time. The new or dark Moon can be very intense
medicine and, when paired with a period, can feel like a lot. Take
care of yourself however you need to: take a ritual bath, make art,
cry, punch or scream into a pillow, lie on the floor and breathe
and scream and cry. Give yourself permission to retreat into your
body.

RED MOON

Those who bleed during the waxing and full Moon follow a "red
Moon cycle." This means that you're the most fertile during the
new or waning moon. This cycle was associated with shamanism,
high priestesses and healers in ancient times, since people who

menstruate during this phase are said to use their darker energies in a more outward way. Instead of turning inward like those with a white cycle, those who bleed during the full Moon may be called to do work around embodiment, creativity and self-growth. The full Moon's potent energy may amplify your feelings during this time, so make sure that you're grounded and supported in your endeavors. Red Moon bleeders tend to use their wisdom to teach others, so channel this and use your passion to help share your love. Lead a Moon ritual, take a ritual bath, create art, go dancing or simply connect with the full Moon to enjoy her energy.

Whether you have a white Moon or a red Moon cycle, there are many other ways to sync yourself to the Moon. Keeping a diary or using an app like Period Tracker can help you get to know your own cycle. By making sure to keep lights on during daylight and off during night, you will help your body get back into rhythm naturally. Spending time under the Moon and taking a Moon bath—like sunbathing, only by the light of the Moon, à la Morticia Addams—is another way to get back in sync with Mama Moon.

Treating your period as a time of sacred renewal and connection can be life changing. Most of us hold a lot of shame around bleeding, thanks to societal stigma. But periods are natural, they're beautiful and they allow us to forge a deeper connection between our bodies and the Moon and natural world. And I think that's pretty special.

the ABCs: crystals and astrology

Crystals and astrology are two essentials in any witch's toolkit. They are a little like building blocks or the letters in the alphabet. Once you're familiar with the energy of the cosmos above and the Earth below, and know their language, you will easily be able to harness the ABCs of crystals and astrology to craft them into your own spells and rituals.

First up, crystals. Crystals are the new black. Walk into almost any shop and you're bound to see a stone like a rose quartz or amethyst either on sale or as a decorative accent. Crystals have emerged as teachers, gifts from the Earth with which we can raise our energy and restore energetic balance. And, of course, crystals do so in the most extravagant and eye-catching way possible.

A crystal is a piece of the Earth's soul in a physical form. You can sense this by looking at one: crystals hold some major power, not to mention striking beauty. To see a crystal is to feel its strength—and that's partly because each crystal is a perfect molecular structure. In fact, they're so perfect that when our auras interact with them, they help to realign our energies. Talk about miracle workers.

Crystals are chambers of wisdom and healing that we can tap into by working with them, or even just by being in their presence. Crystals are as old as the Earth and have evolved alongside her, waiting for us to unlock their potential for healing. Whether you do this by creating an elaborate crystal grid (see page 236) and incorporating stones in your magick, or simply by wearing a jade ring for love is irrelevant; their magick is there, just waiting to be unleashed.

crystals for everyone

There are an overwhelming number of crystals out in the world, so much so that it can be difficult to know where to begin. My suggestion is to find a local gem and mineral store, or a metaphysical shop either online or in real life, and take a look at the stones and see what calls you. Crystals often come to us when we need them, even if we don't know why.

Read the following list to discover some powerful and easily accessible stones to help you start on your own crystal journey.

AMETHYST

Amethyst comes in varieties of purple and lavender shades. One of the most common stones, amethyst is protective and healing, with a high spiritual vibration. It can also be worn to ward off drunkenness and to help overcome addiction, while allowing us access to a higher level of reality. One of the most spiritual stones, it helps to foster our love of the divine, while allowing us to see our true nature. Amethyst also helps to enhance our own psychic gifts and is great for healing of all kinds, for cleansing the aura and for stimulating the throat and crown chakras.

CITRINE

Citrine comes in shades of yellow, yellowish brown and smoky-gray brown, although the yellow-orange variety is the most common. Citrine is like the Sun in crystal form, helping to revitalize, energize and regenerate, while also bringing a sense of warmth to all its healings. Citrine helps with creativity, and since it's a self-clearing stone, it never needs cleansing. This means that it helps clear and cleanse the chakras, especially the solar plexus and sacral chakra. Citrine helps open the crown chakra and intuition and balance the subtle body, and it acts as an aura protector, signaling to us when we need more protection.

CLEAR QUARTZ

Although quartz comes in a variety of shades, clear quartz is exactly that: clear. Clear quartz is one of the most powerful healing crystals out there, and is an incredibly powerful energetic amplifier, enhancing the properties of any crystals used alongside it. Clear quartz works directly with whatever person is using it, taking their energy and restoring it to the most perfect state possible. It helps to cleanse and enhance the physical and subtle bodies, and to connect the mind with the physical domain. Clear quartz contains every color, so it works on all levels. It helps to attune us to our spiritual purpose, and aids concentration and memory. This stone can be used for every kind of healing, and helps to harmonize all the chakras while also aligning the subtle body.

FLUORITE

Fluorite comes in shades of green, yellow, blue, purple and brown, as well as clear. Fluorite is highly protective, and connects the subtle body with the physical body. It helps to clear and stabilize the aura, while guarding against psychic manipulation and outside influences. This stone also helps draw off negativity and stress, and is one of the best stones to use for dealing with disorganization. Fluorite also helps us to connect with the Cosmos, as well as our own spiritual nature, heightening our intuitive powers and accelerating our spiritual awakening. Associated with progress, fluorite can help dissolve unhelpful behavioral patterns and bring our attention to the subconscious, helping us move away from fixed ideas to more fully realize our truth.

GARNET

Garnet can come in a variety of colors, including red, orange, yellow, green, pink, black and brown. Garnet is a powerful energizer that helps rebalance and reenergize the chakras, while also bringing in a sense of power and purpose. Although garnet has long been used for protection, it is also a stone that can be used for issues surrounding love and devotion. For women and femmes, garnet allows us to stand in our power and helps us to let go of shame around speaking our truth. The stone can also be placed on the third eye to help with past-life recall.

JADE

Jade comes in many colors, including cream, lavender, red and white, although it's most commonly found in a green shade. Associated with the heart chakra, jade increases loving and nurturing energies. The stone is said to bring good luck and friendship, and is a symbol of peace, purity and serenity. Jade helps us recognize our spiritual experience as humans in this life, and allows us to integrate this wisdom and connect our minds with our bodies. The stone also helps to soothe the mind and dispel negative thoughts. Green jade specifically can be used to calm the nervous system and harmonize dysfunctional relationships. Physically, it can be used to cleanse the body's filtration organs.

LAPIS LAZULI

A deep blue stone marked with flecks of gold, lapis lazuli (often called lapis) helps open our third eye while balancing the throat chakra. An immensely spiritual stone, lapis can help with dreamwork and developing psychic abilities, spiritual journeying, connecting to spirit guides and harmonizing the body at a physical, spiritual, emotional and mental level. Lapis is also a great leadership stone for women who feel scared when changing from girl to woman. Lapis also helps us find our inner truth and speak it, helping to release anger and any difficulty in communication around the throat chakra. It helps us express our own opinions, while allowing us to confront and acknowledge the truth. The stone encourages creativity and magnifies our thoughts.

ONYX

Coming in shades of black, gray, white, yellow and red, onyx is a powerful stone that helps us to align with our purpose in the world. Onyx helps provide clarity during difficult and confusing times, and it links us with the guidance of our Higher Selves, all while giving us a sense of strength. A stone of connection, onyx can help us see our path forward, providing us with vigor and stamina. Since onyx can become imbued with the energy of its wearer, it can be useful for past-life work, and healing old injuries and traumas. This stone also helps soothe overwhelming feelings

CRYSTALS ARE AS OLD AS THE EARTH AND HAVE EVOLVED ALONGSIDE HER, WAITING FOR US TO UNLOCK THEIR POTENTIAL FOR HEALING.

of worry and fear, while helping to balance the energies in
the body.

ROSE QUARTZ

Coming in shades of pink, there may not be a more loving stone
than this one. A stone of unconditional love, rose quartz helps us
access our heart and keep it open, and is the most important
stone for the heart and the heart chakra. It allows us to access a
space of deep healing and opening, and is incredibly useful for
trauma and crisis recovery. Rose quartz teaches us how to love
more deeply, and can be used to help attract love and romance.
This stone also helps to replace negative energy with loving
vibrations, restoring trust and harmony. Rose quartz helps open
the heart, release grief and transmute hardships and conditioning
that no longer serve us.

TOURMALINE

Tourmaline comes in shades of black, brown, red, yellow, green,
blue, watermelon and blue-green, although the color black is
typically associated with this stone. Tourmaline is a very
protective and healing stone, helping to turn dense energy into a
lighter vibration by cleansing and purifying it. Tourmaline helps to
guard, clear and balance the chakras, and offers protection during
ritual and magical work. Tourmaline can also help you understand
yourself at a deeper level, carving a path for creativity, self-
confidence and self-worth. Black tourmaline is connected with
the base chakra, and helps to ground and clear negative thoughts,
while allowing you to see more clearly.

the stones and the chakras

As you can see in the list above, crystals connect with the chakras. If you remember from Chapter 2, the chakras are the body's energetic centers, each of which corresponds to a specific color and certain properties. If you feel one chakra is out of balance, choose a corresponding healing crystal to meditate and work with. Here's a handy guide to help bring all this information together:

Color	Chakra	Properties of crystal	Stones
Red	Root	Strength, vitality, healing, stimulating, working with anger, passion, grounding and connection.	Ruby, garnet, red jasper, bloodstone and coral.
Orange	Sacral	Energy, self-confidence, sexuality, security, sense of self, eroticism and passion.	Carnelian, topaz, orange calcite, citrine, fire opal and orange jasper.
Yellow	Solar Plexus	Intellect, wisdom, the higher plane, equalizer for the nervous system, creativity, vitality, happiness and fighting depression.	Topaz, citrine, tiger's eye, yellow tourmaline and amber.
Green	Heart	Love, harmony, abundance, creativity, affection, attraction, energy, radiance, universal supply.	Emerald, green tourmaline, malachite, jade, aventurine, moss agate, green jasper, green quartz and labradorite.

Color	Chakra	Properties of crystal	Stones
Blue	Throat	Inspiration, devotion, spirituality, truth, public speaking, sharing and self-expression.	Sapphire, lapis lazuli, blue topaz, aquamarine, turquoise, blue tourmaline and blue obsidian.
Purple/ Deep Indigo	Third Eye	Spiritual attainment, self-mastery, psychic visions, intuition, dreamwork, and channelings.	Sapphire, azurite, purple fluorite and electric blue obsidian.
White/ Purplish White	Crown	Spiritual mastery, spiritual attainment, connection to guides and angels, cosmic consciousness and healing.	Quartz, purple jasper, clear tourmaline, purple sapphire, amethyst and fluorite.

cleansing your stones

Crystals are their own energetic beings that need TLC just like we do. Cleansing a crystal means removing any excess energy that it may have absorbed or clung on to, and clearing it of any energetic impurities. When we cleanse our crystals, we're clearing them so we can work with them, or we're clearing them so they can be charged with an intention.

Thankfully, there are a number of ways to cleanse crystals and I have listed some of the most popular below. Although you can do some of the methods quickly, it's better to honor the practice of cleansing your stones and to take some time to visualize and feel their energy clearing with your mind's eye and your heart. Being in Nature while clearing your stones would be optimal, but this isn't always doable.

» **Using sacred smoke:** you can pass your stone through sacred smoke from sage or palo santo, for example.

» **Moonlight:** leaving your crystals out under the full Moon will not only help clear their own energy, but will charge them with some lunar energy.

» **Water:** using natural water from the sea, a river or a spring would be the best method for this, although tap water will work. Submerge your stone and imagine any energy floating away. (Note: there are some crystals whose properties mean they shouldn't be submerged in water, including desert rose, selenite, tourmaline, calcite, pink Himalayan salt and malachite [for hot water].)

» **Citrine:** as mentioned, this is a self-cleansing stone and placing it around other stones will help to clear and cleanse their energy as well.

» **Burying:** dig a shallow hole and cover your stones in the Earth to help reset their energy.

» **Salt:** leave your crystals in a bowl of salt. (Sea salt and pink Himalayan salt are especially powerful.) However, stones that shouldn't be submerged in water shouldn't be submerged in salt either, including geodes, since these are porous.

» **Sound:** using a gong, singing bowl, bells, chimes, tuning fork or your own voice are all methods of sound cleansing. Clapping at your stones is also a powerful cleanser.

» **Candles:** you can pass your stone through the flame of a white candle to help clear it, doing this quickly so as to not burn the stone. Visualize all the energies and impurities from the stone transmuting into white healing light.

» **Visualization:** holding your stone in your nondominant hand, imagine a white light clearing any negative energy from the stone, and transmuting any impurities into white healing light. Keep imagining this until the stone seems cleansed in your mind's eye.

charging a stone

When you're charging or programming a crystal, you're infusing it with a single intention. You can, for example, charge a crystal for protection, for love, for confidence, for abundance or for tackling a specific health issue. There are probably going to be particular crystals for which you have a certain intention in mind. However, another method is to ask the stone what it wants to help you with. This is especially useful if you pick out a stone intuitively, without quite knowing its innate properties or purpose. First, you can ask a crystal what it would like to help you with, using the Meet Your Crystal meditation on pages 235–36. Then charge it using the following method.

STEP 1: CLEANSE YOUR STONE AND GROUND

Use one of the methods listed above to cleanse your stone, and then ground yourself.

STEP 2: CHARGE IT

Hold your stone in your nondominant hand. Imagine a white light growing outward from your heart until it completely covers you and your stone. Imagine this white light clearing away any negative energy from the stone; this is replaced instead by a white, healing light. Now, inspire your stone with your desired intention or the intention it has suggested to you. Ask for its help, its guidance and its compassion. Hold this as fact in your third eye, feeling your desired intention melting into the stone itself.

STEP 3: GROUND YOUR ENERGY

When you're done, you can imagine all the white light returning to the stone. Ground your energy, either by pressing your forehead to the Earth or by imagining the golden cord from your spine moving back into your body.

STEP 4: WORK WITH THIS STONE

Work with the stone by holding it in your nondominant hand and breathing with it, by meditating with it, incorporating it into spells and rituals or placing it on your altar, bedside table or under your pillow. You can also make art with your stone, charge water with it and simply talk to it.

A MEDITATION TO MEET YOUR CRYSTAL

This powerful meditation was given to me by my friend Momo, and I think it's a wonderful way to get to know your stone, and to hear if it has any intentions and messages for you. You can use any stone for this meditation, but a clear or transparent stone would work especially well.

Pick whatever stone you're charging and hold it in your nondominant hand. Close your eyes and start to breathe and find a connection to the Earth. Once you feel supported and relaxed, imagine that you've shrunk and are standing in front of your crystal. Suddenly, you see a door in its surface. You open the door and enter the stone, where you start exploring it from a multisensory perspective. How does it smell? What does it feel like? Is it cold? Look around: what do you see? Are there any hidden chambers or anomalies in the stone?

After you've explored it, ask the crystal how it would like to help you. Take a moment to see if you feel anything, see or hear anything, or get any other hints or suggestions from it. You can also inspire the crystal with your own intention at this point, asking it to work on your behalf.

Stay here, exploring the crystal for as long as you like, basking in its energy. If you did receive a message on how to work with the stone, acknowledge this and talk to it, letting it know that you received its message and that you'll be working with it in that way, if you desire. Thank the crystal, and then exit through the door. You can return to this meditation whenever you like. If you received a download or intention from your stone, make sure to honor it if it resonates with you. Cleanse your stone regularly and thank it for its love!

A CRYSTAL GRID SPELL TO HARNESS YOUR INTENTION

A crystal grid is a geometric pattern of crystals that uses a central crystal as an energetic focal point. The crystals around this stone charge it with the desired intention, so after the spell is done the crystal is left holding the energy of the entire grid. Search for "crystal grids" online to see exactly how these look.

You'll need: one crystal to act as the central stone; multiple crystals that correspond with your desired intention (at least eight small stones would be preferable). *Optional:* a photo of a sacred geometric pattern.

Step 1: Pick an intention and a central crystal.

Picking an intention and a central crystal are two of the most important aspects of this work. Clear quartz would be a good central stone to work with since it amplifies the energy of the surrounding crystals. Clear quartz is also very easy to obtain and charge. However, you can use any stone you want as the central crystal. This crystal should be cleared and charged with your desired intention for the grid; the more you work with your central stone before this spell, the better. A major reason to do this practice is to continue working with the central stone after you take down the grid, since it will be charged with the energy of the other stones.

Step 2: Ground and center.

Once you've picked your desired intention and your central crystal, it's time to get connected and grounded. Feel the Earth supporting you and visualize the golden cord growing from the base of your spine, down into the Earth. Feel the energy supporting and sustaining you.

Step 3: Set up the grid.

You can set up your grid on your altar, on a piece of paper or on a printout of a sacred geometry pattern or photo. Put your central crystal in the middle of the grid and arrange the other stones around it; while you're doing this, hold each stone in your hand and connect to its energy, reminding it of your intention. You can do this by saying a word to represent your intention, such as "love," "health" or "abundance." Start with stones that amplify the energy of the central stone; more clear quartz crystals and crystal points (i.e., crystals that taper to a point) would work well. However, any stones that amplify your intention would be perfect. If you're working with crystal points, placing them so they point at the central crystal will draw in energy from the Universe, while placing them so the stones point out will help connect the crystal to the Universe's energies beyond it. There is no right way to build a grid, although symmetry tends to work well. Placing stones in the directions of North, East, South and West can also help align the stones with the energy of the Elements. Keep adding stones to your grid while listening to your intuition.

Step 4: Activate the grid.

Once you feel like your crystal grid is complete, it's time to charge it. You can do this by moving your hand around the grid in a clockwise motion, telling the grid to activate itself and finishing at the central stone. Hold your hands here for a second, asking any beings, guides, deities or masters you work with to help activate this crystal with your desired intention.

Step 5: Ground.

After you've activated your crystal, you can ground your energy by pressing your forehead into the Earth or by sitting meditatively. Either way, imagine all the excess energy returning to the Earth and the Universe, where it will honor your intention.

Step 6: Maintain the grid.

Place your grid somewhere it won't be disturbed, like your altar. The more energy you infuse into your grid every day, the longer it will stay active. Keeping up the crystal grid for two weeks would be great, especially from the time of the new Moon to the full Moon. Even if you can't do this, try to keep the grid in place for at least six hours. Once you take your crystal grid down, keep working with the central stone, since the collective energy of the grid will be stored within it. Then, voilà!—you have a new, powerfully charged stone to work with.

astrology

Nowadays it seems like we can barely meet someone without the words "so what's your sign?" slipping out of our mouths. In the past few years, astrology has really gone from being considered a "woo woo" practice to a part of life that many of us take rather seriously. We read our horoscopes, compare our birth charts with our friends' and pay attention to the Cosmos for messages. For those of us devoted to our daily, weekly and monthly horoscopes, however, it's important to remember that horoscopes like these only relate to one part of our birth chart.

A birth chart is like a map of where the major celestial bodies, such as the planets and the Moon, were in the sky at the time when we were born. But when we're reading our horoscopes, we're only reading about our Sun signs, which just relate to where the Sun was when we were born. Since this is only one piece of the puzzle, it makes sense that our horoscopes don't always click. While we have a Sun sign, we also have a Moon sign, a Mercury sign, a Venus sign and so forth. We also have a rising sign, which is what sign the Sun was rising in at the time of our birth. This position changes every two hours, but even if you don't know the exact time you were born, you can still calculate the rest of your chart.

So, as well as being a map of the sky, a birth chart is a personalized blueprint; it's like a cosmic layout that can help us learn about why we are the way we are. However, a birth chart isn't necessarily a guide to your destiny that will predict your future and tell you why things are the way they are. We still have free will, and nothing is written in stone. Instead, the birth chart, like the tarot, acts more like a map to our soul and our true self. It can help explain how you move through this world, and give you insight into unknown parts of yourself, allowing you to understand the way you relate to the world and the people in it. Astrology is less about reading your future and more about revealing your truth.

There are plenty of websites to get your birth chart for free, including astrostyle.com, cafeastrology.com and astro.com. There are also various apps (my favorite being TimePassages) that will help you calculate your chart. Many will give you more insight into your birth chart, and help you learn about what helps to make you, you! Here is a simple birth chart for reference:

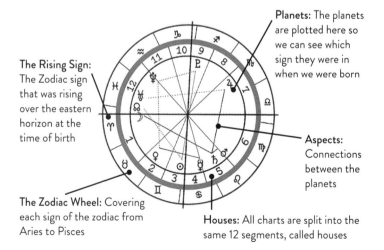

Planets: The planets are plotted here so we can see which sign they were in when we were born

The Rising Sign: The Zodiac sign that was rising over the eastern horizon at the time of birth

Aspects: Connections between the planets

The Zodiac Wheel: Covering each sign of the zodiac from Aries to Pisces

Houses: All charts are split into the same 12 segments, called houses

When you look at the chart, you'll see it's represented by a wheel, known as the zodiac wheel. The zodiac wheel begins at the nine o'clock position (on the left), and moves counterclockwise. The outermost ring on the birth chart is divided into twelve parts: one for each sign of the zodiac. Inside the zodiac is another ring, also divided into twelve sections; each of these is numbered and known as a house. Each house is ruled by the zodiac sign with which it intersects, which means that each house is influenced by the characteristics of that sign. Then, in each house, the various planets and celestial bodies are plotted—and therefore we can also see in which sign they appeared when we were born. Even though the Sun, Moon and North Node aren't technically planets, they're still treated as such by astrologers, and their position in the zodiac holds just as much weight as if they were. The same is true of Pluto, even though it's no longer considered a planet.

My friend Kelsea describes the three main features of the chart perfectly; in her words: "The planets (parts of our nature) are the actors, the signs (what we are like) are their roles and the houses (or areas of our life) are the stage, or scene." Once you learn the basics of each planet, house and sign, you're able to see the ways in which they interact, overlap and relate to one another. Which means you're able to see the ways in which you interact with other people and their birth charts!

This is a really easy and basic way to start to understand your birth chart, but it's just the beginning. There are plenty of other aspects to your chart as well, and astrologers will track the movement of the planets as well as their transits, which is when the planets in their current position move past those in our natal chart.

SOME USEFUL ASTROLOGICAL TERMS

There are certain astrological terms that you will be bound to come across as you go further along this path. Here are a few of the basics to get you started:

» **Aspects:** the connections or relationships between two or more planets.

» **Conjunctions:** when planets are in close proximity to one another.

» **Mercury retrograded:** Mercury, the planet of communication, technology and travel, goes retrograde (see below) for a few weeks at a time, disrupting travel plans, making technology crash and bringing people from our past back into our lives. Retrogrades force us to move intentionally and more slowly. In this case, we need to back up our technology regularly, try to avoid planning any trips or traveling and avoid signing any legal or binding documents or contracts if possible. This also is a time to work on old projects, but not to start new ones. During Mercury retrograde, give yourself plenty of time when traveling and make a conscious effort to move as slowly and intentionally as possible.

» **Retrogrades:** this is when a planet moves past the Earth and seems to be spinning in the opposite direction to the one it normally spins in, making everything the planet rules over go a bit haywire. Each planet has a retrograde, but the one most of us are familiar with is Mercury retrograde (above), which happens around four times a year.

» **Returns:** a transit that occurs when a planet moves back to the position it was in at the time of your birth. For example, a birthday is a solar return, when the Sun is back where it was when you were born.

» **Saturn return:** an intense transit that happens to an individual for the first time around the age of twenty-nine, when Saturn starts to make the journey back to where it was when you were born. The adage of "what doesn't kill you makes you stronger" is true. Saturn returns help you really learn and shape who you are.

» **Squares:** when two planets are at 90 degrees from each other in the circle (of the birth chart).

» **Transits:** when a planet moves past a planet in your birth chart. For example, Saturn is transiting your natal Sun (i.e., Saturn is moving toward where the Sun is in your birth chart).

» **Trine:** when two planets are 120 degrees from each other in the circle of the birth chart.

the zodiac signs

The zodiac signs represent our personality, how we express ourselves and how we show up and relate to the world around us. They're the multifaceted parts of being and self, and they represent how we react and deal with life. Each sign is represented by a symbol or glyph, which is used on the actual birth chart, as well as an archetype that encompasses the energy of that sign.

Sign	Characteristics
Aries (the Ram)	Passionate, entrepreneurial, expressive, energetic, leader and strong.
Taurus (the Bull)	Luxurious, grounded, practical, reliable, stable, loyal, steadfast and sensual.
Gemini (the Twins)	Dualistic, communicative, visionary, thoughtful, adaptable, witty and self-expressive.
Cancer (the Crab)	Sensitive, intuitive, emotional, sympathetic, imaginative, sentimental and romantic.
Leo (the Lion)	Entertaining, dramatic, warm, assertive, spontaneous, generous, broad-minded and outspoken.
Virgo (the Virgin)	Grounded, organized, analytical, logical, intelligent, methodical, practical and adaptable.
Libra (the Scales)	Fair-minded, balanced, tolerant, sociable, diplomatic, easygoing, expressive and caring.

Sign	Characteristics
Scorpio (the Scorpion)	Intense, sexual, transformative, powerful, determined, mysterious and passionate.
Sagittarius (the Archer)	Humanitarian, visionary, expansive, far-reaching, idealistic, generous, enthusiastic and honest.
Capricorn (the Goat)	Disciplined, persistent, practical, methodical, resourceful, responsible and rational.
Aquarius (the Water Bearer)	Original, innovative, friendly, independent, trailblazing, intuitive, intense, humanitarian and progressive.
Pisces (the Fish)	Sensitive, feeling, intuitive, emotional, compassionate, dreamy, artistic, expressive and receptive.

the planets

As mentioned, the planets are like the actors in our lives, each representing a different part of our inherent nature, and each with their own motivation or drive. On top of this, each planet is colored by the characteristics of whatever sign it's in. For example, according to my birth chart, I have my Sun in

Aquarius, so the characteristics of Aquarius (original, innovative, friendly) are expressed through the filter of the Sun (sense of self, inherent nature and self-expression). I interpret this as having an original/innovative form of self-expression, and the reason that I place such an emphasis on being my own person. Again, the planets are the actors in a situation, and the signs are their roles.

In any birth chart, the Sun, Moon and rising signs are key features. While your Sun represents the way you express yourself and move through the world, the Moon represents your inner world and emotions. Your rising sign, which is the sign that was rising on the eastern horizon when you were born, represents the way other people perceive you. Yes, there are many more layers to a birth chart than these features, but these three pieces are very influential, and, at the very least, should make for a good starting point.

Planet	Characteristics
Sun	Sense of self, vitality, our nature, spirit, will, self-expression and creativity.
Moon	Emotions, intuition, what's under the surface, reflection, instincts, responses and needs.
Mercury	Intelligence, how we think, communication, our minds, words, thoughts, writing, speech, logic and ideas.

Planet	Characteristics
Venus ♀	Love, sex, beauty, glamour, aesthetics, harmony, pleasure, passions, creativity and romance.
Mars ♂	Activity, assertion, force, anger, conflict, competition, action and drive.
Jupiter ♃	Generosity, expansion, enthusiasm, fortune, optimism, truth and being outgoing.
Saturn ♄	Structure, discipline, control, wisdom, career, luck, support, boundaries and karma.
Uranus ♅	Awakening, change, innovation, breakthrough, originality, invention and unconventional attitudes.
Neptune ♆	Imagination, mystery, inspiration, intuition, compassion, love, dreams, ideals and fantasy.
Pluto ♇	Transformation, money, death, change, rebirth, drive, fears, renewal and limits of consciousness.

Planet	Characteristics
North Node (where the Moon is in relation to other planets when you were born)	Destiny, personal growth, spiritual growth and karma.

the houses

The houses are like the stage on which the planets and the zodiac signs interact, meaning the energy of both the sign and the planet are ruled by matters connected to that house. The houses represent different parts of our life, much like the suits in tarot. One represents our personality, another our home, another our finances, and so on. Each planet and sign will modify what the house rules over and represents. Plus, each house has its own ruler, which is associated with the energy of the house, called a natural ruler. The first house is associated with the first sign of the zodiac, Aries, the second house with the following sign, Taurus, and so on.

In my birth chart, I have my Sun in Aquarius in the fourth house, which rules over family, home, emotions and habits. I see this as part of the reason why I place such an emphasis on self-nurturing (emotions), having my own space that's unique to me (home) and having a small group of people I'm really close to (emotional habits); Aquarians like to go against the status quo and I've always done this by not having a big group of friends and also by decorating my space like *me*.

Taking a look at your own birth chart and seeing the intersections between the signs, planets and houses will help you grasp the language of astrology. Studying the charts of your bffs or family members will offer you even more insight into this ancient art. As always, dear witch, let your intuition guide you. Your chart won't look like anyone else's (unless you're a twin, like I am!). *No one* knows you better than you do, so trust your gut when you're reading your chart. By seeing how the planets, signs and houses interact, you'll learn not only how to understand your chart, but hopefully how to understand yourself as well.

House	Characteristics	Ruled By
First	Personality, self-interests, leadership, new beginnings, the self and appearance.	Aries
Second	Possessions, personal security, income, money and values.	Taurus
Third	Communication, transportation, siblings, local travel, information and discussions.	Gemini
Fourth	Family, home, parents, the mother, emotions, habits, your "foundation" and the feminine.	Cancer
Fifth	Creativity, love affairs, romance, drama, attention, play, art and entertainment.	Leo
Sixth	Work, wealth, health, wellness, diet, service, organization and routine.	Virgo
Seventh	Relationships, partnerships, contracts, marriages, business deals and social awareness.	Libra
Eighth	Intimacy, sex, death, birth, transformation, mysteries, deep bonding, other people's wealth and possessions.	Scorpio
Ninth	Travel, philosophy, higher education and thinking, long-distance travel, morals and ethics.	Sagittarius

House	Characteristics	Ruled By
Tenth	Public image, structures, corporation, career, politics, responsibilities, the father, awards and authority.	Capricorn
Eleventh	Friendships, service, groups, networking, humanitarian causes, originality and eccentricity.	Aquarius
Twelfth	Inner life, endings, completion, the subconscious, spirituality and spiritual development and the afterlife.	Pisces

CRYSTALS FOR EACH ELEMENT

Each zodiac sign is related to one of the four Elements: Earth, Air, Fire and Water. Working with crystals that correlate to this relationship can help us home in on Elemental energy. For example, depending on where the planets are positioned in your chart and where they fall in relation to the zodiac signs marked around the chart's outer circle, you might find that one of the Elements is underrepresented. (My chart, for instance, means that nearly all the planets sit under signs relating to Air and Water.) If this is the case for you, working with crystals can help to supplement and balance out these energies as necessary.

Besides having an elemental association, each sign can also be labeled as Cardinal, Fixed or Mutable. The Cardinal signs are Aries, Cancer, Libra and Capricorn, who are the initiators of the zodiac and who like to get things going! The Fixed signs are Taurus, Leo, Scorpio and Aquarius, who can be characterized as being firm and dependable. The Mutable signs are Gemini, Virgo,

Sagittarius and Pisces, who are known for being adaptable and knowing how to go with the flow. You can work with the stones associated with the Elements of these signs to tap into their Mutable, Cardinal or Fixed energies as well.

EARTH SIGNS: Taurus, Virgo, Capricorn

Crystals: pyrite, jade, smoky quartz, amber

Earth signs are: grounded, luxurious, practical, stable and loyal.

If the Element of Earth is lacking in your chart, pyrite will help you tap into a structured energy that will allow you to drive your projects forward with gusto and confidence. Jade will help you soften and connect with your heart and your purpose, while bringing you a sense of harmony. Smoky quartz will enable you to connect to your root chakra and, when placed at the foot of your bed, can help your energetic body find some grounding while you sleep. Amber will help cleanse and clear your energetic body, unhooking stuck energy to allow you to reach a more spiritual state.

Other stones to work with: black tourmaline, black onyx.

AIR SIGNS: Gemini, Libra, Aquarius

Crystals: sodalite, moonstone, amethyst

Air signs are: thinkers, creative, communicative, expressive and dynamic.

If the Element of Air is lacking in your chart, sodalite will help you connect to your intuition in an even stronger way, allowing information from a higher plane to access you more easily. Work with black moonstone during the new Moon to manifest your intentions, and white or rainbow moonstone during the full Moon to release and let go. If you've been feeling too trapped in your head or scatterbrained, try working with amethyst to help support your third eye and crown chakra and place a cluster of these crystals in your home to help scatter energy in all directions.

Other stones to work with: lapis lazuli, selenite.

FIRE SIGNS: Aries, Leo, Sagittarius

Crystals: citrine, carnelian, fire opal

Fire signs are: passionate, expansive, visionary, big thinkers, energetic and fiery.

If Fire is lacking in your chart, to help fire up your creativity, revitalize your passions and clear out all the BS, use citrine. This energizing stone will help you burn hot without burning out. You can also work with carnelian to further tap into your root and sacral chakra. Carnelian will help you find grounding in the present, while inspiring your creativity and revitalizing your aura. Fire opal will enhance your personal power, helping you to navigate any intense changes you're going through. This stone will also help you to let go of and burn through any feelings you've been storing up, making way for new, fresh ones to arrive.

Other stones to work with: garnet, clear quartz.

WATER SIGNS: Cancer, Scorpio, Pisces

Crystals: rose quartz, blue lace agate, kunzite

Water signs are: feeling, intuitive, sensitive, emotional and dreamy.

If the Element of Water is lacking in your chart, tap into the well of your emotions by working with rose quartz or rose quartz–infused massage oil. Rose quartz will allow you to explore your emotional needs, while kunzite will help you with unconditional love and awakening your heart. Kunzite will also help protect you from unwanted negative energy. Blue lace agate will enable you to speak your truth, while offering calm and a sense of peace. This stone will also help you calm any feelings of anger, while you find a new mode of expression that better serves you.

Other stones to work with: lapis lazuli, fluorite.

Well, you're officially on the way to learning the language of the stars! The good news? It only gets more fun from here. As you continue to explore astrology, and your own birth chart, you'll start to see your true self illuminated more and more. It's not that who you are will suddenly change; instead you'll have a better understanding of what helps to make you, you. You'll also have greater insight into why you do things the way you do. And beyond this, you'll hopefully understand your place in the grand scheme of things a little more clearly. Astrology won't predict your life, but it can most definitely help you to plan your destiny by showing you fresh sides of yourself, as well as revealing your fullest potential.

Another advantage of astrology? It can help you relate to and understand other people in a more holistic and compassionate way. Soon you'll get why your mom with her Leo Moon isn't as receptive to your emotions as someone with a Cancer Moon might be. And you'll understand why, when you're giving a presentation to the boss who's a Virgo, you'll need to be extra organized and analytical.

If you keep studying astrology, soon you'll be asking everyone for their birth information so you can draw up their chart. And when you do, you'll have a better understanding of the way you relate to them on an emotional, physical and spiritual level. Astrology acts like a bridge connecting all of us, because in the eyes of the Cosmos, we're all the same and we all come from the same star dust. Yes, the shape that stardust takes might look a little different in each of us; but if we learn how to identify and work with those differences, we're much better off and able to see all the ways in which we're actually the same.

May astrology help you find compassion and empathy for others, and for the way in which you relate to the world around you. May it help you learn the best way to communicate with the important people in your life. May it help you learn about your own style of being and doing. And more than anything, may it help you make a little more sense of the world around you.

not your grand-mother's grimoire

In this chapter, you'll find some basics about different forms of magick you can experiment with, ritual and spell outlines and tables of correspondences so as your craft develops, you can begin to create your own distinct brand of magick. This section will guide you in writing your own spells and rituals and combining herbs, crystals and candles so you can create a grimoire customized for your own form of witchcraft.

May it help inspire you and lead you further on your path of witchiness! As always, listen to your heart and intuition and see what feels right. Honor your own path, practices and passions to craft a magick that's tailored to you.

a basic ritual outline

Rituals serve a variety of purposes, but mostly they are a way to connect us to something bigger than ourselves. There is comfort in ritual, and knowing the steps can allow us to be even more present in what we're doing, allowing us to connect to the Universe more completely. There are rituals for love, for abundance, for protection, for healing, for everything; and each culture, each tradition, each country, each family and each person will have their own specific set of rituals. Creating one of your own, with which you work regularly, is a really important way of curating your own magick.

Here's a basic outline that you can adapt for your own wants and needs. Maybe you don't need to cast a circle or invite the Elements in each time, or maybe your work is honorary and you don't need to release a cone of power. Maybe you ground, cast a circle and then make art. However you go about it, the aim of ritual is to connect you with your intention, while connecting with your own power and the power of the Universe. That's it. Ask yourself what you need, what your magick needs and what the most powerful process will be for you—and then go there.

Create your own basic ritual outline in your grimoire and add in details as you go. You'll have something to look back on in a year as a baseline of how your magick has grown and evolved. And you'll have your own personal ritual practice to turn to again and again.

STEP 1: PREPARE YOURSELF AND THE SPACE

This can be by burning palo santo, frankincense and sage, cleaning, wiping everything down with Florida or flower water, sprinkling salt in the corners, using holy water or sweeping with a cinnamon broom. This is also when you prepare your altar and place any talismans, crystals, herbs or other correspondences you need for your work on it. You should also prepare yourself: you can take a ritual bath or shower, put on certain clothing, take clothing off, put on certain perfume, smudge yourself with sacred smoke and do whatever you need to get yourself in the magick space.

STEP 2: GROUND AND BREATHE

Connecting to the Earth and the breath is always an important way to center our energy and allow ourselves room to create magick. You can ground your energy as described on pages 29–30.

STEP 3: CAST THE CIRCLE

Casting a circle of protection will not only protect you, but it will create a safe container for all the energy you raise, so that when you release that energy it will be potent and powerful. You can walk around and use an athame or wand to cast your circle, as described on pages 45–47, or you can imagine a sphere of protection growing from your heart and encompassing your space.

STEP 4: INVITE IN THE ELEMENTS

You can call in the Elements, as described on page 41, setting up your altar to face North, and calling in the Element for each direction: North/Earth, East/Air, South/Fire, West/Water.

STEP 5: INVITE IN WHICHEVER DEITIES, GUIDES OR BEINGS YOU WORK WITH

You can call in any specific ancestors, gods, goddesses, masters, faeries—or whoever else you work with at this time.

STEP 6: STATE THE INTENTION

During sabbat celebrations, often the intention or myth of the holiday is read out or stated. You can likewise state the intention of your ritual if you wish.

STEP 7: PERFORM THE MAGICK

If you're performing a spell, working with divination, meditating, creating art or whatever else, now is the time to do it.

STEP 8: RAISE THE CONE OF POWER

Once your magickal working is done you'll want to raise energy to release. You can do this by chanting, dancing, doing vinyasa yoga or doing anything that raises the energy up. Once you feel the energy is at its peak, imagine a cone facing upward, with its base at your circle of protection. This funnels all the energy upward, releasing it into the Universe so your magick can manifest. Stay with this energy for a few breaths.

STEP 9: DISMISS WHATEVER DEITIES, GUIDES OR BEINGS YOU INVITED

Thank them for lending their energy to your ritual.

STEP 10. DISMISS THE ELEMENTS

If you worked with the compass directions and the Elements, move counterclockwise around your circle, starting with West/Water and then dismissing South/Fire, East/Air and finally North/Earth.

STEP 11: CLOSE THE CIRCLE

If you walked the perimeter at the start of your ritual, walk it again in a counterclockwise direction, imagining the energy of the circle moving back up through your arm, through your heart, through your feet and back into the Earth. You can say, "The circle is open, may it never be broken," once you're back at the front of the circle. If you did the sphere visualization, imagine the sphere returning into your heart, flowing down the base of your spine and back into the Earth.

STEP 12: GROUND BACK INTO THE EARTH

Press your forehead and palms back into the Earth, and imagine any energy that wasn't released into the Universe is now moving back toward the core of the Earth so she can manifest it. Once the ritual is done, eat something, drink some water and enjoy!

DIY spellcraft

Spells are personal; even if you cast the same spell as someone else, yours will probably look and feel different. After all, if you're unlike anyone else, why would your spell be any different? One of the best parts of spellwork is that we can customize and write spells for ourselves when we need to. I like to think of this as being the all-you-can-eat buffet of spellwork: you pick the means to the end (a plate or a bowl), the main, the side dishes and the drink. The same is true of magick: you'll pick a method (e.g., candle or sigil magick), the stuffing (the correspondences you use) and the toppings (any chants or magick you pair with it). You can eat this like tapas or have a complete meal (a quick spell versus a full ritual).

how to write your own spell

Use the questions below to help you concoct and customize your own spell in no time.

1. WHAT ARE YOU TRYING TO DO?

Are you trying to attract, banish, create boundaries—or something totally different? Get clear about what you want out of this spell.

2. WHAT KIND OF MAGICK DO YOU WANT TO PERFORM?

Are you trying to work with candle magick, sigil magick, sex magick, visualization, body work, energy work or something else entirely?

3. HOW CAN THIS SPELL REPRESENT YOUR OUTCOME?

Get creative! If you're trying to protect yourself from someone abusive, maybe draw a protective sigil over a map of your area. If you're hoping to banish a feeling, think about burning it away. If you're planning to attract love, think about how you can give the love you want to yourself. If you're doing a spell for a specific person or thing, what can you use to represent them? If you're trying to cleanse, how can you incorporate ritual handwashing or a bath into the spell? Try brainstorming a few ideas to get inspired. You can create a multiple-step spell this way too if there are different things you're trying to do.

4. WHAT CORRESPONDENCES DO YOU NEED?

Think about the candle colors you can use; what oils you can anoint yourself and your candles with; any herbs you can burn or incorporate into the magick; any tarot cards that represent your outcome; any crystals that will help channel the energy; any things like hair, clothing or belongings you can use to represent someone in a binding spell, etc. Are you calling in any faeries, deities, masters or other beings? Are there any spirit guides or animal spirits you can work with? Think about this like a project you're creating; what can you use to further explain the message? Using Pinterest, technology, cutouts, photos, magazines and icons can all be useful. Once you know the intention behind your spell and you have a better idea of what kind of magick you want to perform, use this chapter and the correspondence table to help you pick out specific energetic allies you can work with.

5. WHAT WILL YOU BE SAYING?

Think about your intention, and how you plan on translating that through the spell. An easy way to do this is to include a verbal charm to accompany it. Take some time to write this down, experimenting with prose and poetry and different beats. You'll want to make this as clear and intentional as possible to call in what you're asking for. Take into account the steps you'll be taking and if you can say multiple things throughout. If this is going to distract you from the magick you're working on then maybe say something simple or nothing at all. If you like you can write your charm and display it in your grimoire on your altar or work space.

6. HOW CAN YOU PLACE THIS IN THE CONTEXT OF A LARGER RITUAL?

Once you have the basis of the spell, think about the larger ritual. Will you be cleansing yourself as part of the spell? Will you want to take a ritual bath? Will the way you're raising the energy impact the spell?

7. WHEN WILL YOU PERFORM THE SPELL?

Keeping in mind the intention of the magick, now's the time to pick a day and a Moon phase on which to perform it. Remember that from the new to the full Moon we manifest, and from the full to the new Moon we banish. If you can, working a spell on a new or full Moon would be best. Use the correspondence table to pick a specific day on which to work your magick.

8. WILL YOU BE WEARING ANYTHING SPECIAL?

Last but not least, think about what you'll be wearing. Will you be working skyclad, i.e., nude? Or do you have a special dress or cloak you can use? You can even buy something you only wear for ritual and spellwork if you desire.

Once you have all this figured out, record it in your grimoire and get to work. Recognize that spells take time to work, and allow at least two to four weeks for it to really settle in. Take notes of any outcomes.

A NOTE ON LOVE MAGICK

I know, I know—it can be so tempting to craft a spell to get your crush to love you. The thing is, has this ever worked? Well, not for long. As much as it sucks, and as frustrating as it is, performing love spells on people is a big no-no. With free will, and the possibility of everything going wrong, it's better to just avoid it. Instead, when crafting love spells and love magick, think about the traits and characteristics that you'd like to find in somebody.

Look at your favorite couples and ask yourself about the dynamic you're looking for. What is it that your soul and heart desire, and what are they longing to feel? Casting spells using this sort of approach is bound to bring you something even better than any particular individual you might have wanted to cast the spell on.

candle magick 101

Candle magick is a practice that can be incorporated into other energetic and magickal workings. You can use this guide to help you pick certain candles for spells, and to help you figure out how to dress them.

For candle magick, the color of the candle, the oils and herbs you use to dress it and the way you put on the oil are all significant. You can mix and match the following suggestions to suit your own candle-dressing situation. Use these in conjunction with "How to Write Your Own Spell" on pages 263–67 and "A Basic Ritual Outline" on pages 259–62 and you can create your own rituals.

STEP 1: PICK THE COLOR OF YOUR CANDLE

White will always work and is good to use when you don't have a lot of supplies, or simply want to attract positivity and protection. For more specific purposes, consider the following:

Color	Meaning
Red	Passion, sexual love, health and fire.
Pink	Love, femininity, nurturing, protection of children and healing the heart.
Orange	Encouragement, creativity, stimulation and attraction.
Yellow	Creativity, vision, illumination, positivity, purpose, the Sun, logic
Green	Finance, luck, wealth, prosperity and fertility.
Blue	Tranquillity, patience, healing, the ocean and femininity.
Purple	Royalty, magick, power, ambition, business progress, spirituality and connection to your Higher Self.
Black	Absorbs negativity; darkness and night.
White	Attracts positivity; healing, light and purity.
Silver	Moon energy and protection.
Gold	Wealth and abundance.

STEP 2: PICK YOUR OIL

You can always use olive oil to dress your candle, although there are plenty of other oils available in metaphysical shops, like love oil, candle-dressing oil or essential oils.

STEP 3: PICK YOUR HERBS

Although it's optional to dress your candles with oils and herbs, herbs do add some extra energy and will make your spell more powerful. See the Tables of Correspondence on pages 274–77 to help you decide which essential oils and herbs to use for your magick.

STEP 4: DECIDE HOW TO DRESS
THE CANDLE

Anointing with oil: For spellwork designed to attract, dress the candle with the oil by moving from the top to the middle, and then the bottom to the middle. To banish, dress the candle with oil by moving from the middle up to the top, and then from the middle to the bottom of the candle.

Writing on the candle: You can also write your statement or intention, or a sigil (like we did on our shoes in page 161), on the candle using a toothpick, pen or needle. If you're writing a statement, follow the same procedure as for dressing it with oils, moving from the top to the middle and then the bottom to the middle to attract; and moving from the middle to the top and then the middle to the bottom to repel.

Herbs: Sprinkle your herbs of choice in the same way you wrote and anointed your candles. Make sure you cover the candle on all sides with the herbs and oils, but you don't have to go too overboard with herbs.

Pair with a written intention if you like: Once your candle is dressed, you can pair it with a written intention. Write down your intention beforehand, then light your candle, read out the intention, fold up the paper and place it in front of the candle. Focus your energy on your intention as the candle burns.

sex magick 101

Sex magick is an umbrella term for a type of magick that works with sexual energy (like orgasms) as a form of magick and energy release. As you'll notice in this book, I mention using masturbation as a way to harness and release energy for spell and ritual work; this is a form of sex magick. Contrary to popular belief, sex magick isn't all about orgies with the devil under the full Moon! Sex magick utilizes sexuality, but this doesn't necessarily have to involve having sex. It can be magick surrounding any sort of sexual energy and sexual exploration. This will mean different things for different people, just like sex itself—and that's totally okay!

The most popular way to work with sex magick is through masturbation. Masturbation is not only totally normal and natural, but something most of us do anyway. Sex magick gives this a little twist. By masturbating while concentrating on manifesting something, you're charging energy (your orgasm) with intention. And this is especially effective when used in conjunction with a magickal working such as a spell as a way to raise the cone of power. Though orgasm is the goal with this practice, the raising of the energy is the most important part. Even if you don't achieve orgasm, the energy is still potent.

And even if you're not working with sex magick in this way, you can still utilize this practice by exploring your own body and whatever sexual energy means to you. You can even create a ritual out of this, allowing yourself to breathe and feel deeply as you take your time exploring what feels good and what doesn't. This can be its own form of energy release, and one into which you can ease at your own pace. Like any other aspect of the craft, allow this to unfold naturally. And don't forget—you don't ever have to do anything you're uncomfortable with.

HOW TO MAKE HOLY WATER

Holy water is energetically charged salt water that is used to cleanse and clear energies and spaces. It can also be used to call in the Elements, to represent the ocean, to cleanse ritual tools and to anoint people.

You'll need: a chalice; salt in a small bowl or dish; water; an athame—or your fingers!

Step 1: Fill your chalice with water and connect.

Fill your chalice with water; spring water works best but filtered or tap will also do. Start to breathe, imagining the water as perfectly clear, vibrant energy.

Step 2: Add three pinches of salt.

Using your athame, or your fingers, put three small pinches of salt into the water.

Step 3: Stir clockwise (deosil).

Using your athame or your finger, stir the water in a clockwise direction until the salt starts to dissolve; stirring in multiples of three is best. As you do this, imagine the water going from a clear color to a vibrant, bright white. Once you've stirred, hold your palm over the cup and say:

> *"I cleanse and consecrate this holy water in the name of the Universe and my highest power."*

Hold this white, healing energy in your mind for a few more breaths until you feel it in your body.

Voilà! Holy water! You can sprinkle this in front of your door for protection, in the corners of your house to cleanse it, over your altar tools to cleanse and consecrate them, and you can anoint your third eye with it to help you channel its energy. You can also use this water to call in the Elements and to charge it under the Moon to create Moon water. Use it in rituals when you need to cleanse and in spells when you need some extra protection.

cleansing ritual items

Cleansing items like an athame or a wand is a way to clear their energy, like smudging. You can do this when you first get the item, and whenever you feel like it needs to be cleared. Performing this practice at the sabbats or esbats would be perfect.

You can say:

> *"I cleanse and consecrate this [say your ritual item] in the name of the Universe and my highest power."*

while doing one of the following:

» Smudging with the smoke of frankincense (which you can burn on a hot coal to keep the smoke going if you're not using sticks of incense).

» Sprinkling holy water on the ritual item.

» Passing the item through sacred smoke.

» Calling on the Elements and cleansing the item with their assistance, while using holy water and sacred smoke to cleanse and consecrate it.

» Leaving it under the full Moon and placing selenite and citrine around it.

tables of correspondences

Magickal correspondences are based on the notion that everything has an energetic signature of sorts, which makes it suitable for being worked with in a particular way. If you become familiar with the correspondences of colors, crystals and days of the week, for instance, you'll be able to harness this knowledge in your spellcraft and make your magick even more powerful by working with energetic allies that help you work toward your desired outcome.

Your grimoire will also grow as your magick grows. Allow your magickal diary to expand, and enjoy the process of adding to it. Like your practice, your grimoire won't look like anyone else's. Whether you use yours as a way to record your dreams and hopes for your magickal journey, or for recipes and spells, it will evolve just like you. Enjoy the journey, and don't forget to take a second to record your process every now and then.

Correspondences of Herbs

Purpose	Herbs
Love	Herbs of Venus, acacia flowers, jasmine, lavender, mistletoe, myrtle, valerian, vervain, violet, rose, gardenia, apple and cinnamon.
Protection	Basil, feverfew, hyssop, laurel, motherwort, nettles, patchouli, rosemary, rowan, sandalwood, frankincense, myrrh, cinnamon, vervain, sage and bay leaves.
Healing	Carnation, rosemary, gardenia, garlic, ginseng, hops, mint, saffron, rowan, rue, eucalyptus and peppermint.
Psychic Work	Dragonwort, mugwort, ginseng, laurel leaves, saffron, chamomile, dandelion, skullcap, catnip, clover, mint and nutmeg.
Manifesting	Bamboo, beech, dandelion, ginseng, pomegranate, sage, sandalwood, violet and walnut.
Creativity	Laurel, lavender, cinnamon, myrtle, valerian and orange.
Banishing/ Binding	Nettle, devil's shoestring, bamboo, benzoin, cayenne, rosemary, sage, frankincense, mandrake and peppermint.
Wealth	Balm, High John the Conqueror root, lavender, mandrake, oak leaves, saffron, valerian, mint, cinnamon and sage.

Correspondences of Weekdays, Planets, Colors, Crystals, Elements and Herbs

Day	Associations	Planet	Color	
Mon	Magick, mystery, illusion, Divine Feminine, emotions, travel and fertility.	Moon	White, silver.	
Tues	Strength, courage, passion and the energy needed to face a challenge.	Mars	Red	
Wed	Communication, writing, change, knowledge and teaching.	Mercury	Violet	
Thurs	Prosperity, abundance and health.	Jupiter	Deep blue and royal purple.	
Fri	Love, healing, beauty, glamour, sex and fertility.	Venus	Green, indigo and pink.	
Sat	Protection, banishing, karma and cleaning up.	Saturn	Black, blue and dark purple.	
Sun	Success, wealth, career and fame.	Sun	Gold and yellow.	

Crystal	Element	Herb
Moonstone, pearl and clear quartz.	Water	Chamomile, cucumber, mushrooms, pumpkin, seaweed and wild rose.
Bloodstone, garnet and ruby.	Fire	Basil, coriander, dragon's blood, ginger, garlic, mustard and onion.
Opal and agate.	Air and Water	Carrots, dill, fennel, lavender, parsley, pomegranate and valerian.
Amethyst, sapphire and turquoise.	Air and Fire	Ash, clover, dandelion, juniper berries, mint, nutmeg and sage.
Amber, emerald and rose quartz.	Earth and Water	Apple, fig, mint, mugwort, raspberry, rose, strawberry and violet.
Pearl, onyx, obsidian, hematite.	Earth and Water	Hemp, marijuana, poppy, patchouli, thyme and yew.
Topaz and yellow diamond.	Fire	Chamomile, citrus fruits, St. John's wort, sunflower, rosemary, marigold and rue.

in conclusion

So, beloved witch, I hope you have found some solace in these pages. I hope they've helped ignite and spark your spirit, sending you on a path of true magick; and that in this book, you've found a piece of your soul, a piece of your potential, a piece of the wildness that lives inside of you. My biggest hope is that you've been able to feel into your own personal, perfect, unlike-anyone-else's path of the craft. That you've been able to honor the feelings that are leading you to your own brand of magick. My wish is that you've been able to feel your intuition guiding you forward to whatever comes next on your journey and that you honor this by following and listening to the call.

I also hope that these pages have empowered you to stand as your truest self. There are infinite paths of witchcraft and magick, but the only one that matters is the one you're on. May you honor those who come before you; may you honor your ancestors; and may you honor yourself through your practice. And may you remember that you're always welcome to revisit this book whenever you need.

Your energy is sacred, your energy is powerful and your energy is transformative. May you never forget who you are: an incredible, powerful, worthy witch. May your magick grow as you do. May it evolve as you do, and may it help you bring a deeper sense of purpose and meaning to everything you do. With a blessing from the Earth and the Cosmos, with a blessing from me to you, with a blessing from the Universe, find your magick, find your path—and know in your bones that it is your truth.

FURTHER READING

Ahlquist, Diane, *Moon Spells: How to Use the Phases of the Moon to Get What You Want* (Adams Media, 2002)

Beyerl, Paul, *A Compendium of Herbal Magick* (Phoenix Publishing, 1998)

Chocron, Daya Sarai, *Healing with Crystals and Gemstones* (Samuel Weiser, Inc., 1986)

Cunningham, Scott, *Magical Herbalism: The Secret Craft of the Wise* (Llewellyn Worldwide, 2017)

Dale, Cyndi, *The Subtle Body: An Encyclopedia of Your Energetic Anatomy* (Sounds True, Inc., 2009)

Farrar, Janet, and Stewart Farrar, *A Witches' Bible: The Complete Witches' Handbook* (Phoenix Publishing, 1984)

Gillett, Roy, *The Secret Language of Astrology* (Watkins, 2012)

Hall, Judy, *The Crystal Bible: A Definitive Guide to Crystals* (Godsfield Press, 2003)

Mayo, Jeff, *Teach Yourself Astrology* (Hodder & Stoughton, 1998)

McCoy, Edain, *A Witch's Guide to Faery Folk* (Llewellyn Worldwide, 2003)

Murray, Margaret Alice, *The Witch Cult in Western Europe* (FG Classics, 2007)

Starhawk, *The Spiral Dance* (HarperOne, 1999)

U.∴D.∴, Frater, *Practical Sigil Magic: Creating Personal Symbols for Success* (Llewelyn Worldwide, 2015)

Warrington, Ruby, *Material Girl, Mystical World* (HarperCollins, 2017)

Wintner, Bakara, *WTF Is Tarot?: . . . & How Do I Do It?* (Page Street Publishing Co., 2017)

ACKNOWLEDGMENTS

This book is dedicated to all the witches before me who have allowed me to be here.

It truly takes a village, and I'm lucky enough to have a village of strong, powerful, astonishing women behind me. But I couldn't start the acknowledgments without first thanking all the witches who came before me who have allowed me to be on this path and share it freely and fiercely.

Infinite thank-yous to my literary agent Jill Marr at Sandra Dijkstra Literary Agency, and Nina Shield and the whole TarcherPerigee team who have made the experience of writing my first book unforgettable. To my family for all their love and support over the last decade of witchery; I wouldn't be who I am without you. To my mother for first introducing me to spirituality and glamour magick, to my father for fostering my love and curiosity about the unknown, to my twin sister, Alexandra, for always supporting me and for taking the incredible photos in this book. You three have been the best support system a soul could ask for and I love you all to the Moon and back. To my Tita (and Tito) for always loving me as my truest self and for supporting me. To my Grandpa Harry, who I know I would have loved and made sex jokes with. To my Grandma Rose, who I'll never have enough words to thank, and also for her love of words and fashion magick that I carry with me every day. To Marissa Patrick, my twin flame and best friend who has been there with me every step of the way. To my Auntie Melissa who started me on this path, who I wouldn't be here without. To Sheryl Rachmel, for being the best therapist and helping me through the process of writing this book and embracing my voice and gifts. To all the incredible editors and teachers who have led me here. To Ruby Warrington and The Numinous for helping me find my voice and magick and for always believing in me and giving me a chance. To the whole *HelloGiggles* team for the support and encouragement. To Marty Preciado for reminding me of my power, and believing in me fiercely and endlessly. To NYLON, Gabrielle Korn and Kristin Iversen for giving me a chance and seeing my potential as a witch and giving me a platform to share my vision. To my coven. To Alexandra Roxo for reminding me of my power, strength and innate divinity. To Kaitlyn Kaerhart for always seeing my truest self and reminding me of the importance of my words and soul. To Ivory Woods for being the best friend, fashion fairy godmother and supporter of me and my journey I could ask for. To Amelia Quint for being my astrologer witch queen and Amanda Sharpley for being my supporter and creepy gal advocate, and for being my coven on the East Coast. To Miranda Feneberger, Kelsea Woods, Ashley Laderer and Hayley Francise whose love and support have helped me come into my own since the very beginning. To my OG family and friends in California who have always supported me in being my truest self. To Taylor "Bruja" Cordova for the beautiful smudges and love and support. To Momoko Hill for the crystal wisdom, love and sweet soul that always knows just what to say. To J. K. Rowling for the witches who have inspired me to be confident in my own magick. To all the Twitter and Instagram friends and witches who I've met along the way and have changed me for the better, and for all the love and support of my journey.

Also by

GABRIELA HERSTIK

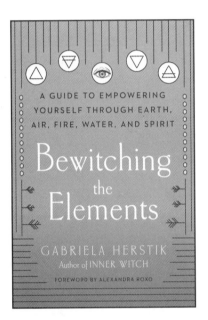

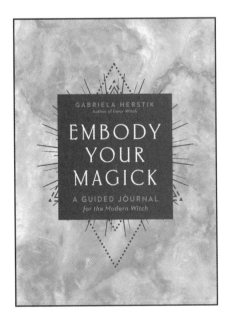